100
FUN & EASY
LEARNING GAMES

TEACH READING, WRITING, MATH AND MORE WITH FUN ACTIVITIES

FOR KIDS

AMANDA BOYARSHINOV & KIM VIJ

certified teachers and creators of
TheEducatorsSpinOnIt.com

PAGE STREET
PUBLISHING CO.

First published in 2016 by

Page Street Publishing Co.

27 Congress Street, Suite 103

Salem, MA 01970

www.pagestreetpublishing.com

Distributed by Macmillan, sales in Canada by The Canadian Manda Group.

19   18   17   16   1   2   3   4   5

ISBN-13: 978-1-62414-196-6

ISBN-10: 1-62414-196-X

Library of Congress Control Number: 2015953174

Cover and book design by Page Street Publishing Co.

Photography by Ashlee Hamon

Printed and bound in China

Page Street is proud to be a member of 1% for the Planet. Members donate one percent of their sales to one or more of the over 1,500 environmental and sustainability charities across the globe who participate in this program.

DEDiCATION

From Amanda

To E, N & W—may you always enjoy learning.

From Kim

To my children—you are my everything. Your spark for knowledge is the fire behind my joy of teaching.

CONTENTS

INTRODUCTION

This book is a collection of hands-on, skill-based learning games that are easy to make, using materials you can find around your house, and are fun to play. Each game is designed to keep your child busy, happy and learning.

Yes, learning can and should be fun!

Choosing the book *100 Fun & Easy Learning Games for Kids* clearly shows that you believe education is important.

Children can play these learning games with an adult or another child to race the clock, complete a task or compete for points. Each game includes easy-to-follow directions to make and play. They are designed to reinforce and extend reading, mathematics, science, art, social studies, writing and music concepts that are typically introduced to children in the early-childhood years.

As the parents of children ages 2, 4, 5 and 8, we wanted to make sure that the skills our children worked so hard to learn would be remembered. We also wanted to extend our children's learning and challenge their thinking in fun ways.

We are not alone in wanting to provide our children with educational activities. Throughout the many playdates we have attended, we hear a common theme: Parents are looking for fun ways to engage and teach their children. We have looked through teacher manuals and parenting books to find activities that were not only fun, but correlated with the academic standards taught within the education curriculum.

Although written specifically for families to play with their children during the day and after school, these games are also good for childcare providers and school teachers as well.

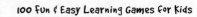

Enrich Your Child's Academic Learning with Free and Low-Cost Learning Games

Classroom teachers have a lot of academic content to pack into every learning day. No matter how amazing your child's classroom experience is, most children need to practice and extend learning beyond the classroom to solidify math concepts. If the learning is not reinforced, it may be forgotten. Games are a great way to reinforce and teach academics in a fun and exciting way. No worksheets or flashcards are needed.

Learning games are adaptable to meet the needs of all learners. These games are great for gifted learners to challenge and extend learning. These games are also great for students who are struggling to master academic concepts and need additional practice on the fundamentals of education. We have provided three variations for each game to meet the needs of your child throughout various stages of learning.

Simple is best. Some of these learning games and concepts may seem simple. They are. We often make things harder than they need to be. But the reality is, simple is easy to make and do. Simple activities take less time to prepare and are easier to include in your everyday activities. Parents and teachers like simple.

Kids like simple, too. It is easier for kids to focus on a few academic skills at a time. Although each activity includes variations, try only one of them every day, or even every week.

Keep it simple and everyone will be happier!

Benefits of Playing Games

Playing games has many benefits for children. Games are a great way to learn life lessons, such as sharing and taking turns. They require children to practice waiting and observing what others do. They are also a great way to practice being a winner.

Children may not naturally demonstrate that ability. As parents and teachers, we must model the appropriate behaviors and discuss how to be a good sport.

The games in this book will also allow children to practice, strengthen and extend their academic learning in a fun and exciting way.

Teacher Talk with Amanda and Kim

Designing a Playful Learning Environment

Amanda: It is important to have a clean space set aside for learning. This can be in one area in a room or spread out in several spaces throughout your home. We like to use baskets and bins to store toys and learning materials. Think about the places where your child may use the particular materials and place these storage containers nearby.

Kim: Having a designated space helps to set the mood and expectations for your child. Establishing times of the day can help keep you motivated as a parent to set aside time to focus on your child's learning.

Amanda: We use a special space in our room for story time. It has a soft rug for the children and a place to prop up books and charts for reading. My kids know it's reading time when I sit on the rug and sing the alphabet. It is our signal that learning time is about to begin and they race over to join in.

Kim: Providing age-appropriate toys, games and materials at eye level for kids helps build a sense of independence and allows them to build skills of self-choice and responsibility for things.

Emphasizing Early Literacy

Amanda: Every early-learning space needs an alphabet chart. This chart can be handmade or store bought. I like ones that show both the capital and lowercase letters as well as a picture to represent each letter. Labeling the materials and stations in your room is also a way to encourage early literacy. The light switch, for example, may have the word light written nearby. As you leave the room, point to the word and say "light." These words can be referred to as environmental print.

Kim: Having writing materials readily accessible helps to build a print-rich environment. Keeping word lists and magnetic letters up on the fridge encourages your child to build words and express the importance of print. Making lists, reading, writing labels and modeling with your child can help to build a strong literacy foundation.

Amanda: One year, we made a word list every day for 26 days. I wrote the words and they drew the pictures. We hung them up on our window ledge so they were low enough for the kids to read. The kids interacted with these words more than our store-bought alphabet chart because they were meaningful to them.

Kim: We use our everyday tasks and adventures to make handmade books together. When they were younger, they would tell me what they did and I typed or wrote the words, and then we illustrated together. As they've grown, they've begun to write and illustrate their own stories to create keepsakes from our adventures at home together.

Amanda: I put books everywhere. There are books on famous buildings in our block area. There are cookbooks in our pretend kitchen. There are train books in our toy train container.

Kim: We look to books to help solve questions and learn about new topics. Reserving books online at a library on a specific topic is one of my biggest tips for handling the library with younger children. My kids handpick a few of their choice books and then I pick up the reserved ones at checkout.

Organizing the Space

Amanda: Children need to have a space to work. My kids rotate between the floor and child-size table and chairs. Offer a variety of rugs, cushions for the floor and small chairs. Make the space inviting by using primary colors and a variety of textures.

Kim: Learning environments work best when they are consistent. To keep them exciting, rotating activities will help to encourage engagement. Learning zones work even better for the youngest learners. Consider using a bookcase set up with trays and bins that contain games and materials, with a table just for them nearby.

Amanda: We have found that limiting the number of materials available to children helps keep the learning space more organized. Although we have a variety of building blocks and materials to use with kids, we may only have one type available for kids to play with. The others are stored in a closet and will be rotated out several weeks later.

Kim: Setting up a box or basket in a special spot that has a theme is one of my favorite ways to group toys, games and books together with younger kids at home. It helps keep me focused as a parent on goals we're working on together at home.

Encouraging Creative Exploration

Amanda: I believe every learning environment needs a space for children to express their creativity. We have a designated area on tile with wipe-able walls for art exploration. Paper, crayons and glue are accessible at all times. Messier items such as paint, beads and play dough, are stored out of children's reach and are brought down for play with adult supervision.

Kim: We have a craft cart with drawers in which we store all of our art materials. Stored on top is an art tray that is used to transfer items to the table and allow projects to sit on to dry or be completed. Inside our art cart there are items like markers, crayons, glue, scissors, paint, stickers, sequins, stencils, stamps, glitter and lots of paper choices. I set aside times each week to be sure I take it out and encourage my kids to create something that's self-chosen. Don't get rid of those diaper wipes just yet; as they grow up, keep them handy for doing messy projects with paint, finger paint and glue.

Amanda: We have a designated area for children to display their artwork and projects. It is simply a rope with clothespins. A bulletin board or magnets on the side of a fridge work well, too.

Kim: Sending art projects off in the mail can be a fun way to connect with family members who live far away. We're working on creating a digital library of the kids' art projects over time. Consider printing it out in a collage format to hang up and celebrate their creativity.

50 Things Kids Learn in an Early-Childhood Education Environment

Preparing children for success in school is one of the top priorities for parents. Knowing what the expectations are for your child can help make supporting your child in school easier. Listed below are some common goals that we see throughout the stages of early childhood education. These are skills that are being introduced, practiced and mastered in a variety of settings based on a child's prior knowledge and experience. Children can develop at different rates, but the goals remain common for all.

Here are 50 goals we hope you work towards as you and your child play the games in this book.

1. Writes first and last name with first letter uppercase and the remaining lowercase.
2. Uses scribbles, shapes and letter-like symbols to write words and ideas.
3. Uses pictures to communicate ideas.
4. Knows the letters in the alphabet, both uppercase and lowercase.
5. Identifies all the letter sounds.
6. Says letters in alphabetical order.
7. Rhymes words.
8. Identifies parts of a book.
9. Knows beginning concepts of print.
10. Blends sounds together to make words.
11. Blends and isolates syllables in words.
12. Identifies basic sight words.
13. Identifies beginning, middle and ending sounds in words.
14. Tells, draws and writes a story using 3 to 5 sentences.
15. Begins to write complete sentences with punctuation and capital letter.

(continued)

16. Sequences events and life cycles.

17. Groups and sorts items by similarities and differences.

18. Recognizes simple patterns and duplicates them.

19. Identifies basic two-dimensional geometric shapes.

20. Demonstrates concepts of positional words.

21. Counts objects one by one up to 10.

22. Identifies numbers 0 to 10.

23. Counts to 30.

24. Estimates number of items in a group.

25. Tells which number comes before and after a given number to 30.

26. Skip counts by 10's, 5's and 2's.

27. Identifies coins and their value.

28. Understands concepts of time.

29. Solves basic addition and subtraction problems.

30. Uses standard and nonstandard units to measure.

31. Knows all of the basic colors.

32. Recognizes uses for maps and globes.

33. Understands that the Earth is made from different landforms.

34. Has an awareness of their self within continents, countries, states, cities and home.

35. Knows that there are a variety of people, objects, music and holidays around the world.

36. Understands what nutritional food is and where it comes from.

37. Observes and identifies changes in surrounding environment.

38. Works to identify problems and uses critical thinking skills to solve them.

39. Demonstrates the skill to observe and vocalize observations.

40. Identifies and expresses emotions of self and others.

41. Creates a self-portrait with proper body parts.

42. Uses various materials to create representations of objects.

43. Listens to and sings songs with others.

44. Identifies various types of music and instruments.

45. Uses appropriate three-finger grasp with writing materials and scissors.

46. Cleans up after playtime.

47. Follows directions.

48. Identifies and respects differences and similarities in others.

49. Communicates and shares with others.

50. Knows that they are loved.

HOW TO USE THIS BOOK

Each day have your child play a learning game in one subject area. You can start on one topic and play one game each day, or select a game based on the academic skill your child is working on. The activities vary in level of difficulty. Many of the game variations will provide options to make them easier or more difficult depending on the academic level of your child.

Create a small area of your home where you can store learning supplies. This space can be a small basket or plastic container. We like to put the games and supplies into individual bags within the container. This helps keep them in good condition for reuse and makes it easy to grab a game and play. If a particular game is a favorite of your child's, consider laminating it for longer use.

 Some children learn best through movement. The active learning games are marked with a shoe. This shoe will indicate to you that the game involves gross motor skills. Play these games between stationary activities to allow children the opportunity to move and wiggle throughout their day.

 Often families are on-the-go, running errands or driving to sports or art classes. There are games that require little or no supplies that you can play while in the car or sitting at the doctor's office. Most of these games target auditory learning, meaning they require children to use hearing to play. These games will have a car to indicate they are easy to play while on-the-go.

Disclosure

This book is intended to be used as a way to enhance a child's learning environment. It is not intended to replace a curriculum. You know your child best and how he or she interacts with materials; please observe caution and safety at all times. All activities are intended to be used with adult supervision. Appropriate caution should be used when activities call for materials that could be potentially harmful, such as scissors, or items that could present a choking risk (small items) or a drowning risk (water activities). The authors and publisher of *100 Fun & Easy Learning Games for Kids* disclaim liability for any mishap or injury that may occur from engaging in any of these activities in this book.

FANTASTIC READING

Oftentimes, we think of beginning reading only as learning the alphabet. Although learning to read does include the knowledge of letters, it encompasses so much more. These games include everything from letter names and sounds to learning sight words and extending sentences. The following games touch upon just a few components of early literacy and are a great way to reinforce and teach early-reading concepts.

It is recommended that in addition to playing a learning game with your child each day, you also read to your children for 10 to 15 minutes. Discuss the story with your child. Talk about the characters, setting and storyline. Talking about the story strengthens reading comprehension and vocabulary. We have found that the best times for reading stories are:

★ First thing in the morning

★ Right after lunchtime

★ After dinner

★ Before bedtime

Make sure to read a variety of fiction and nonfiction books, allowing your child to self-select the books they are interested in. Trips to the local public library or bookstore will help increase the number of books in your home library and encourage more reading.

COMMUNITY CORNER

How did you teach your child the letters of the alphabet?

"To me, teaching letters needs to be meaningful to kids. So I love starting with their names and other names that are important to them (friends' names and family members' names), along with environmental print. I also like capitalizing on how much children want to tell you the stories behind their drawings and artwork—this aligns with teaching writing, as well."

—Mary C.

"I have a habit of saying the letter and sound that accompanies the letter, 'OH, look, that's a BIRD—B—buh, buh, BIRD.' It annoys my son, who is now 9, but our preschoolers LOVE it and chant along. I SING most everything to our kids."

—Darla H.

"We read a book with letters in it and when he asked, 'What is that?' I told him the letter."

—Cerys P.

"My oldest son learned his letters through lots of playful games and activities. ABC puzzles and magnetic letters were two manipulatives we used regularly during our play."

—Jodie R.

"Honestly, with my first two, I worked and went to school, so they learned in a home daycare. With my last two, well, I'm currently exploring with them. We play lots of games and random daily learning through life."

—Natasha J.

"We had an alphabet book and we read it to our son every night before bed. We would point to the letter on each page and say the name of it, and then have him repeat it. First he memorized the names of the letters, then we started working on the sounds they made. He was around 2 when we started that."

—Samantha V.

"I'm not sure that I've ever purposefully taught them."

—Kim S.

"We played games where I deliberately said the wrong letter and sounds and she would say, 'Mommy, no, that's wrong.'"

—Alecia F.

"I used a whole language approach. If we were out at the grocery store and we saw a sign for milk, we traced the letters with our fingers. If we were out for a walk, we played 'I spy' as we walked by signs and billboards."

—Dayna A.

STACK A WORD

Learning to read can be exciting for children. Learning how to blend letter sounds is one of the foundations to success. Players use movement and visual clues as they stack the cans to form words.

Focus Skill: blending letter sounds in spoken words

Great For: moving while you learn

Materials

Construction paper

Scissors

10 cans of similar size

Black marker

Tape

Directions to Make

1. Cut 10 papers to wrap around the cans.
2. Write two vowels and two consonants on each paper. Vary letter combinations to include all letters.
3. Attach a letter paper to each can with tape.
4. Write down on a separate paper select consonant-vowel-consonant (CVC) words in focused word families.

Directions to Play

1. One player calls out words from the focused word family sheet.
2. The other player uses the cans to sound out the words and stack on one another to form each word.
3. Continue to create words until all the cans are used.

Game Variations

★ Use cans to create letters in family members' names.

★ Create word family sets by adding an additional vowel-only can.

★ Create nonsense words and sound out while stacking on top of each other.

ROLL THE ALPHABET

Children often can sing the alphabet, but have trouble saying it. The letters *l, m, n, o, p* are separate letters. These letters are the building blocks for literacy; naming the letters is one component. So, grab a ball and get rolling. See if you can get from A to Z without letting the ball roll away!

Focus Skill: saying the alphabet in order

Materials

ABC chart or poster

Playground ball

Directions to Make

1. Prior to playing, sing the ABC song with your child.
2. Show your child the alphabet poster. Sing the song again and point to each letter as you sing it.

Directions to Play

1. Have the child sit on the floor with their feet touching yours. Explain that you are going to say a letter and roll the ball to them. Roll the ball to them and say "A."
2. They will say the next letter in the alphabet and roll the ball to you.
3. Continue the game in this manner until you reach the end, Z. Try to roll the entire alphabet without having the ball roll away.
4. Move further distance apart from each other and repeat the game.

Game Variations

★ As children become more confident with rolling the ball, try to bounce the alphabet.

★ For an extra challenge, say a word that begins with that letter. Apple, bear, coin, dog...

★ Roll the letters in the child's name.

MYSTERY ALPHABET

Everyone loves a good mystery. In this game children will close their eyes and take turns being a letter detective by feeling the shape of the hidden letter. This game teaches children to be more aware of the shape of each letter. Knowing the shape of the letters will help children transition to reading as they see these same shape formations within books.

Focus Skill: identifying lowercase letters

Great For: on-the-go learning

Materials

ABC puzzle

Small paper or canvas lunch bag

Directions to Play

1. The first person will place a letter in the bag while the other will close his or her eyes.

2. Put your hand in the bag to feel the letter. NO PEEKING!

3. Try to guess the letter name and say the sound the letter makes.

4. Take the letter out to check if your guess was right.

5. If you guess right, then it is your turn to select the next letter. If your guess was wrong, close your eyes and let the first person select another letter.

6. Continue the game until all the letters have been identified.

Game Variations

★ Instead of saying the letter name and sound, have the child say a word that begins with that sound. If the letter is M, they may say, "Monkey starts with m."

★ As the letters are pulled out of the bag, arrange them in alphabetical order.

★ Use a shape puzzle in lieu of letters for a shape math game.

Note

All children learn differently. Activating the sense of touch is different from relying on eyes. When you are playing learning games with your child, make sure to include a variety of senses. Take note of which activities your child tends to enjoy more. Do those often!

ZIP-LINE LETTERS

Zoom the alphabet across the room in this high-flying zip-line adventure. Uppercase letter names and sounds are traditionally taught first. If your child has mastered the uppercase letters, then consider writing all lowercase or even making a set of both and matching the letters before zooming.

 Focus Skill: letter identification, letter sounds

Great For: moving while you learn

Materials

2″ (5-cm) tag board squares (one piece of paper will make 20)

Black permanent marker

Paper clips

Tape

15′ (4.6 M) of yarn

Directions to Make

1. Write one uppercase letter on each tag board square until all the letters have been used.

2. Bend the paper clip to create a hook.

3. Tape the paper clip hook to the back of each letter square, making sure that one half is sticking out of the top of the square.

Directions to Play

1. Tie one end of the yarn to a solid stationary object, such as the handle of a closed door. Hold the other in your hand.

2. Slide a letter card and hook onto the yarn near your hand. Pull the yarn tight.

3. Raise your arm and watch the letter soar.

4. As the letter zips across the room, make its sound. Example: BBBBB, MMMMM or ZZZZZZZZZZZZZZZZZ!

5. Build another zip line parallel to the first.

6. Invite a friend or family member to race letters.

Game Variations

★ String the letters on in order or zoom your name.

★ Put three or more letters together on the zip line to spell a word.

★ Pictures with beginning word sounds can zip after the letters.

SQUIRT THE LETTER FISH

Learning letter sounds is a splash with this outside water game. Young children need to interact with letters in a variety of ways. This will help them gain familiarity with the way each letter looks and sounds. The goal is for children to see a letter and be able to name the sound instantaneously. If they can name the sound after thinking about it for a while, that is fantastic. Keep playing with the letters to speed up the recognition!

Focus Skill: identifying the most common sound for the letters

Great For: moving while you learn

Materials

Chalk

Spray bottle or water bottle with water

Directions to Make

1. Chalk the outline for 26 fish on the driveway or fence.
2. Write a letter inside each fish.

Directions to Play

1. Call out a letter sound, such as B, that is heard at the beginning of the word big.
2. Have your child spray the letter fish that makes the sound.
3. Continue to call out letter sounds until all have been identified.

Game Variations

★ Call out the letter name instead of the letter sound to work on letter identification.

★ Use letter cards and have the child first draw a letter from a bucket and find its match to squirt.

★ Call out a word and have your child spray the letter fish that makes the first sound in that word.

STRINGING LETTERS

Memorizing the shapes of letters will quickly help your child learn to identify the alphabet. Players create fun, hands-on letters using glue and string. Once ready, they make the perfect material to hang in alphabetical order for even more letter practice.

Focus Skill: identifying alphabetical order

Materials

Yarn

Scissors

Wax paper

Glue

Container

Sturdy rope

26 clothespins

Directions to Make

1. Cut yarn into pieces of various lengths.

2. Lay out wax paper on a smooth surface for letters to dry on.

3. Have children dip yarn pieces into glue container and then shape wet yarn into letter formations on the wax paper.

4. Allow yarn to dry before playing the game.

5. String a long and sturdy rope up in the room and attach clothespins onto it.

Directions to Play

1. Players work together to place letters in alphabetic order by attaching them to the rope with the clothespins.

2. As they place the letters, encourage them to name the letters they are attaching to the rope.

Game Variations

★ Use letters to create a child's name on the rope.

★ Use letters to create sight words.

★ Create a timed challenge to see how fast they can put letters up in alphabetical order.

Note

This game needs to be created over the course of a few days to allow for drying. Consider starting with the letters in a child's name or a specific grouping of letter formations, like E, L, T, I, H.

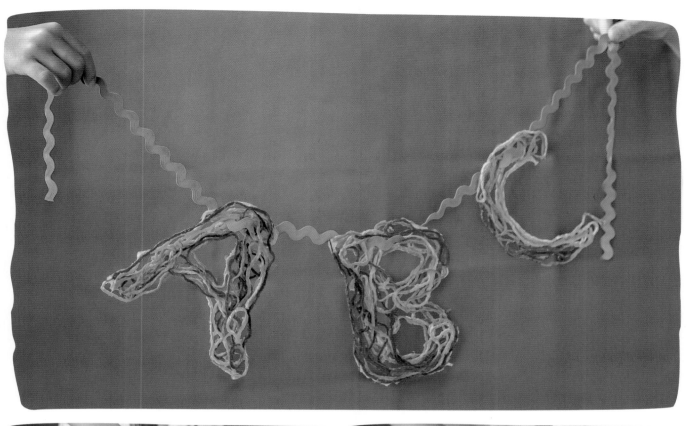

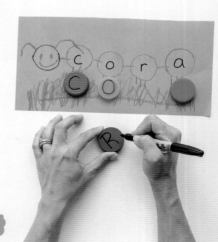

CATERPILLAR COVER

Children of all ages are fascinated with both caterpillars and colorful lids. Gather your recyclables to make and play this eco-friendly game. Your kids will have a blast practicing letter matching with a little fine motor strengthening too.

focus Skill: matching uppercase and lowercase letters

Materials

10 or more plastic lids

Printer paper

Pencil

Crayons

Permanent marker

Directions to Make

1. Trace the lids onto the paper to make circles for the caterpillar's body. Make one caterpillar for each player.
2. Draw a face and antenna on an end circle. Color and add legs to the caterpillar.
3. Write one lowercase letter inside each remaining circle.
4. Write one uppercase letter on each plastic lid.

Directions to Play

1. Turn the lids upside down.
2. Flip one lid. Read the letter, then place it on the caterpillar, covering its lowercase pair.
3. Repeat until the caterpillar's body is filled.

Game Variations

★ Make the caterpillar the same length as your child's name. Write the letters in the circles and on the lids.

★ Make several caterpillars for focus on sight words or spelling words.

★ Use number words in the circles and dots to represent the numerical amount on the lids.

1, 2, 3, LET'S FIND THE A, B, C'S

In this spin-off the classic hide-and-seek game, children search for letters and place them in alphabetical order as quickly as possible. It's a great game for rainy days, to get kids moving and learning the letters.

 Focus Skill: knowing the letter names in order

Great for: moving while you learn

Materials
14 (3" x 5" [7.5 x 13-cm]) notecards

Scissors

Black marker

String

Directions to Make
1. Cut each of the notecards in half.
2. Write one letter of the alphabet on each card. Make sure to use all capital letters or all lowercase letters.
3. Lay the string straight on the ground.

Directions to Play
1. One player hides the alphabet cards in the selected area while the other players close their eyes.
2. When all the cards are hidden, the players open their eyes and say, "1, 2, 3, Let's find the A, B, C's."
3. As they find each letter, they bring it back to the string on the floor. They say the name of the letter and place it in alphabetical order. Use the string alphabet from Stringing Letters (page 24) as a guide.

Game Variations
★ For advanced learners, have the children say the name of the letter and name a word that begins with that sound.
★ Swap words in a sentence for letters and have the children search for and build a sentence.
★ Instead of hiding the letters around the room, place the letters in a sensory bin to find.

LETTER TOSS RACE

Who can find and name the letters of the alphabet the fastest? Challenge your child to name and toss the letters of the alphabet with this playful alphabet movement game. This game is a fun, hands-on way to focus on learning letters and letter sounds with your child.

Focus Skill: recognizing uppercase and lowercase letters and sounds

Great for: moving while you learn

Materials

Index cards

Black marker

Alphabet stickers (optional)

Foam, wooden or plastic letters

Bucket

Directions to Make

1. Create letter cards for the game by writing each alphabet letter on a card. Optional is to use alphabet stickers to add color. Complete with your child.

Directions to Play

1. Lay out the plastic letters of the alphabet for players to select from.
2. Set up the letter cards and bucket within tossing distance of the letters.
3. One player holds up the letter card.
4. The second player identifies the letter and finds it in the plastic letter pile.
5. The second player then tosses it into the letter bucket by the other player.

Game Variations

★ Create cards with images that represent each letter sound and ask players to locate and identify the letter to be tossed.

★ Create cards with lowercase letters and allow players to only choose from uppercase letters in pile to play.

★ Use two buckets and two sets of letters for players to race to find the letters the quickest, with one person holding the cards for players.

BUILD A LETTER

What are letters made of? Sticks, circles and curves of course! This game is perfect for your little engineer who likes to build things. Make a set of shapes and then have your child pick three and see which letters they can make. Our favorite letter is Q because it uses two curves and a short stick. Which letter is your favorite?

Focus Skill: identifying uppercase and lowercase letters

Materials

Cardstock or cereal boxes

Ruler

Scissors

Paper

Marker

Game Variations

★ Build a shape.

★ Make a pattern with the pieces.

★ Use all of the pieces to build simple consonant-vowel-consonant words.

Directions to Make

1. Using the cardstock, cut two each of:
   a. Rectangles ½ inch x 3 inches (1.3 x 7.5 cm)
   b. Rectangles ½ inch x 6 inches (1.3 x 15 cm)
   c. 6-inch (15-cm) circles
   d. 3-inch (7.5-cm) circles with middles removed
   e. 6-inch (15-cm) ovals cut in half with middles removed

2. Write the alphabet (uppercase or lowercase letters) in order on the piece of paper to use as a reference and a game recording sheet.

Directions to Play

1. Pick three shapes from the pile.
2. Build a letter.
3. Put an X over the letter on the alphabet.
4. Put the pieces back into the pile.
5. Repeat steps 1 through 4. See if you can build all the letters in the alphabet.

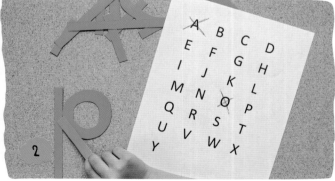

SLIDE AND SAY

Next time you are at the park, bring along some alphabet letters to play this word-blending game with your child. The kids LOVE sliding letters down the slide and making new words. Learning at the park just feels inherently more playful! This game is a great way to combine gross motor movement, outside play and reading.

Focus Skill: blending single-syllable words

Great For: moving while you learn

Materials

Letters from a puzzle

Directions to Play

1. Set the alphabet pieces out at the top of the slide.
2. Call out a single-syllable word. Sample words: red, hit, hot, cut, cup, mat, rug.
3. Have the child select the letters needed to make the word.
4. Encourage them to say the letter sounds as they slide each down the slide.
5. The child then slides down and says the word as they slide.
6. The letters are collected and brought back to the top.

Game Variations

★ Slide a single letter, saying the sound as you slide.

★ Write entire sight words on note cards, slide and say the words.

★ Use numbers instead of letters. Slide the number. Then you slide. When you get to the bottom, hop that many times.

STAR HOP

Much of traditional learning seems to take place in a desk. Although important, it's also vital to get kids moving and shaking. This sound game will encourage children to pay extra attention to the middle sounds in words. Driveway reading is always a favorite at our house!

Focus Skill: isolating and pronouncing middle sounds in simple three-letter words

Great For: moving while you learn

Materials

Sidewalk chalk

List of consonant-vowel-consonant (CVC) words (sample words: cat, dig, bag, rig, bet, fig, red, man, bug, ten, run, can, let, fit, mat)

Directions to Make

1. Clean an area on a sidewalk or driveway.
2. Draw a straight line that is 6 feet (1.8 M) long.
3. Draw a 6-inch (15-cm) circle, star and another circle 2 feet (60 cm) apart on the line.
4. Write the word "start" 1 foot (30 cm) before a circle.

Directions to Play

1. The child stands on the word "start."
2. The parent or teacher calls out a CVC word.
3. The child then hops on the circle and calls out the first sound. They then hop on the star and call out the middle sound. They hop on the second circle and say the last sound.
4. The parent or teacher points to the star and asks, "What sound did you hear in the middle of the word?" The child then calls out the star sound. If needed, encourage the player to re-hop the word.

Note

Being able to identify the middle sound in words is often harder than finding the initial or ending sounds. Use a suggested game variation or switch the star to the beginning or ending of the line for a while before focusing on the middle sounds.

Game Variations

★ Write the CVC words on 3-inch x 5-inch (7.5 x 13-cm) notecards. Have one child call out the words for the others to hop.

★ Leave a bucket of chalk at the end of the line. Encourage the players to hop the sounds then write the word on the sidewalk.

★ For extra support, work with one or two word families at a time. Slowly add in words as each sound is mastered.

FiLL THE BUCKET

Toys and learning tools are all around you. Use them in a new way in this early-literacy game that focuses on isolating initial, or beginning, sounds in words. The kids always look forward to a friendly race to fill the letter buckets. Set out a few small restaurant toys and your kids are sure to find a few items for each letter... Okay, who are we kidding? You have our permission to skip the hard ones! *Unless, of course, you have a zebra in your house.*

Focus Skill: initial letter sounds

Great For: moving while you learn

Materials

Plastic letters or homemade letter cards

Bag or container for letters

3 plastic buckets or containers

Small toys or objects

Directions to Make

1. Place the plastic letters or letter cards in the bag or container. Mix.

Directions to Play

1. Select three letters from the bag. Read the letters selected. Say the name and the sound the letter makes.

2. Set one letter in front of each bucket.

3. Race around the room to find small toys and objects that begin with that letter. If B was selected, you may add a ball, bear, bat, bag or banana to the bucket.

4. When the game is over, dump the buckets out and name the objects. Remove any that do not start with the selected letter. Then count the number of objects in each bucket. The letter with the most WINS!

Game Variations

★ Use colors instead of letter sounds.

★ Pre-select the objects for the three letters and have the child race to sort them into the buckets.

★ Vary the number of buckets from 1 to 5, using fewer for younger learners and more for an added challenge.

ABC WATER CHALLENGE

How fast can you find a letter sound? With this sound challenge players quickly search for the letter sounds that are being called out. Knowing the sound each letter makes is phonics, and vital to being able to sound out words. Letter sounds are the foundation of early reading for kids.

Focus Skill: identifying most frequent letter sounds

Materials

Foam letters

Container big enough to fit the foam letters

Water

Water-friendly vertical surface

Alphabet chart

Directions to Make

1. Create a setup for letters to be placed on a vertical surface.

2. Create or purchase foam letters.

3. Set up the container with water for letters.

Directions to Play

1. One player or adult calls out the letter sound from the letter chart.

2. The second player locates the letter in the water and places it on the vertical surface.

3. The game continues until all the letter sounds have been called and placed on the surface.

Game Variations

★ Set a time and see how fast each player can find the letter sounds.

★ For younger children, start with a smaller amount of letters and letter sounds.

★ Create images for each letter sound for players to use to find a match.

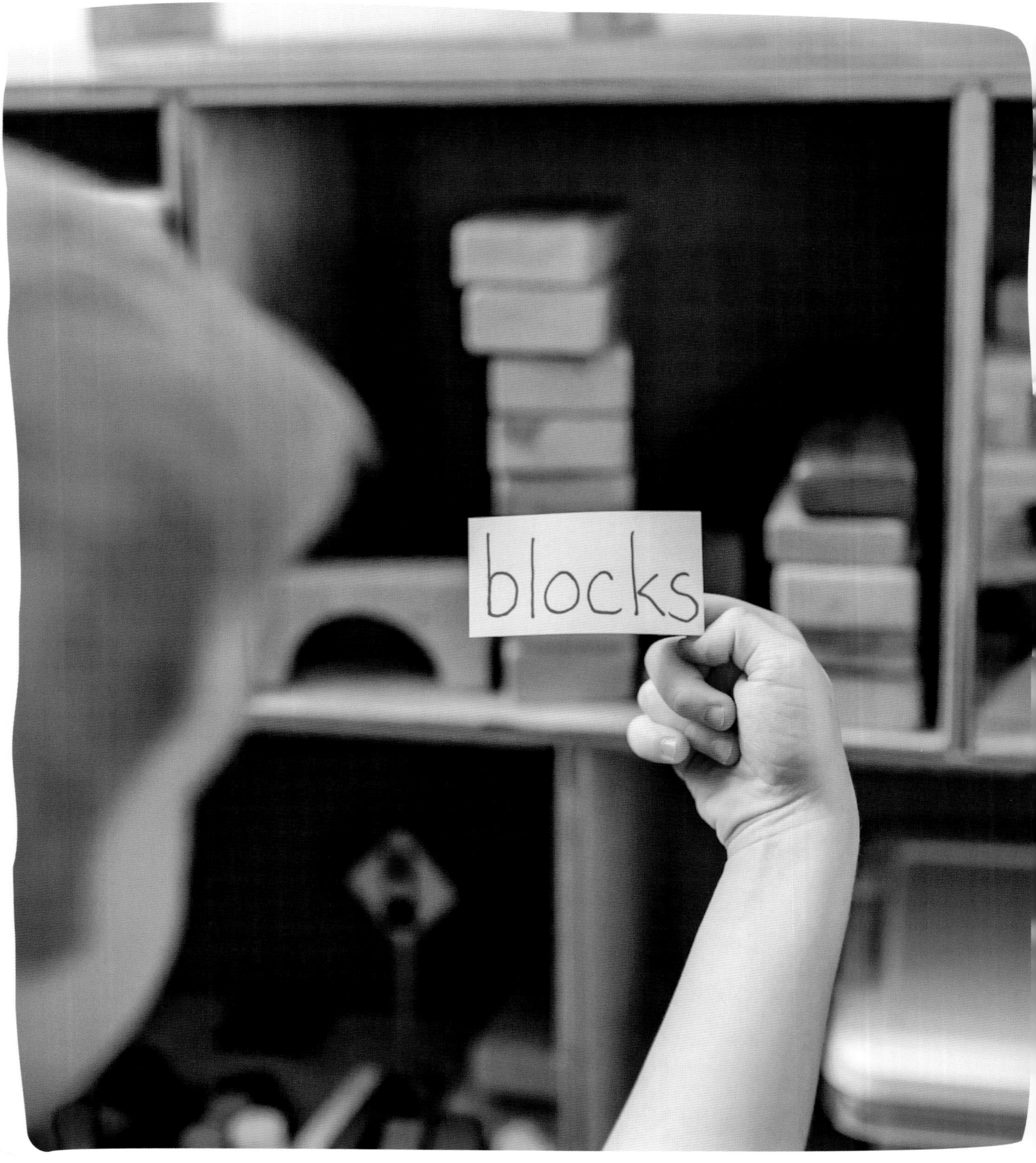
blocks

LABEL THE ROOM

What does this word say? In this reading game, children race to label the objects in the room with words. Not only is this a great way to learn new words, it is a fast way to add more environmental print to your learning area. Environmental print words are those your child sees in their world. These words must be taught and used on a day-to-day basis for them to be most effective.

Focus Skill: reading simple words

Great for: moving while you learn

Materials

3" x 5" (7.5 x 13-cm) notecards

Marker

Painter's tape

Timer

Directions to Make

1. Select 10 objects in your learning area. Write the word or phrase of each object on a notecard.
2. Roll up tape and stick to the back of each word card.

Directions to Play

1. Put five cards on the fingers of one hand.
2. Read the words on the cards.
3. Have the child place all five cards next to the object they represent. Don't give any hints!
4. Walk around and read the cards out loud. Celebrate if the word is in the correct place. Allow the child to re-place the card if it is not labeled correctly.

Game Variations

★ Include a picture sketch next to each word.

★ Write a full sentence on each card.

★ Make a chart with all of the words used. Match the word card to the chart prior to placing it next to the object it represents.

FAMILY PHOTO WORD PUZZLES

Family names are often the first words our children learn to say, read and write. Use your digital images in a new way by creating fun, hands-on family photo puzzles your child will love. As they piece together the pictures of family members, they will begin to practice word recognition of their names, too.

Focus Skill: word recognition

Great for: on-the-go learning

Materials

Camera

6 to 10 printed 4″ x 6″ (10 x 15-cm) photographs of family members

6 to 10 squares of 6″ x 6″ (15 x 15-cm) construction paper

Scissors

Ziplock bag

Game Variations

★ Create additional photo word cards for household objects or favorite animals.

★ Create letter puzzles by taking photos to represent each letter of the alphabet.

★ Write a sentence under each picture.

Directions to Make

1. Encourage your child to take photos of family members.
2. Select photos of each family member to print.
3. Glue each photo onto a piece of construction paper, leaving a 2-inch (5-cm) space below the photo.
4. Write family members' names or key words below the photos, making sure to leave space between each letter.
5. Cut each image into vertical puzzle pieces, with one letter on each piece.

Directions to Play

1. Place the photo pieces with letters into the bag.
2. Take turns drawing puzzle pieces from the bag. As your child removes the piece they will arrange pieces into the proper letter order to create the word.
3. Once assembled, encourage your child to practice naming the words and letters in the family members' names.

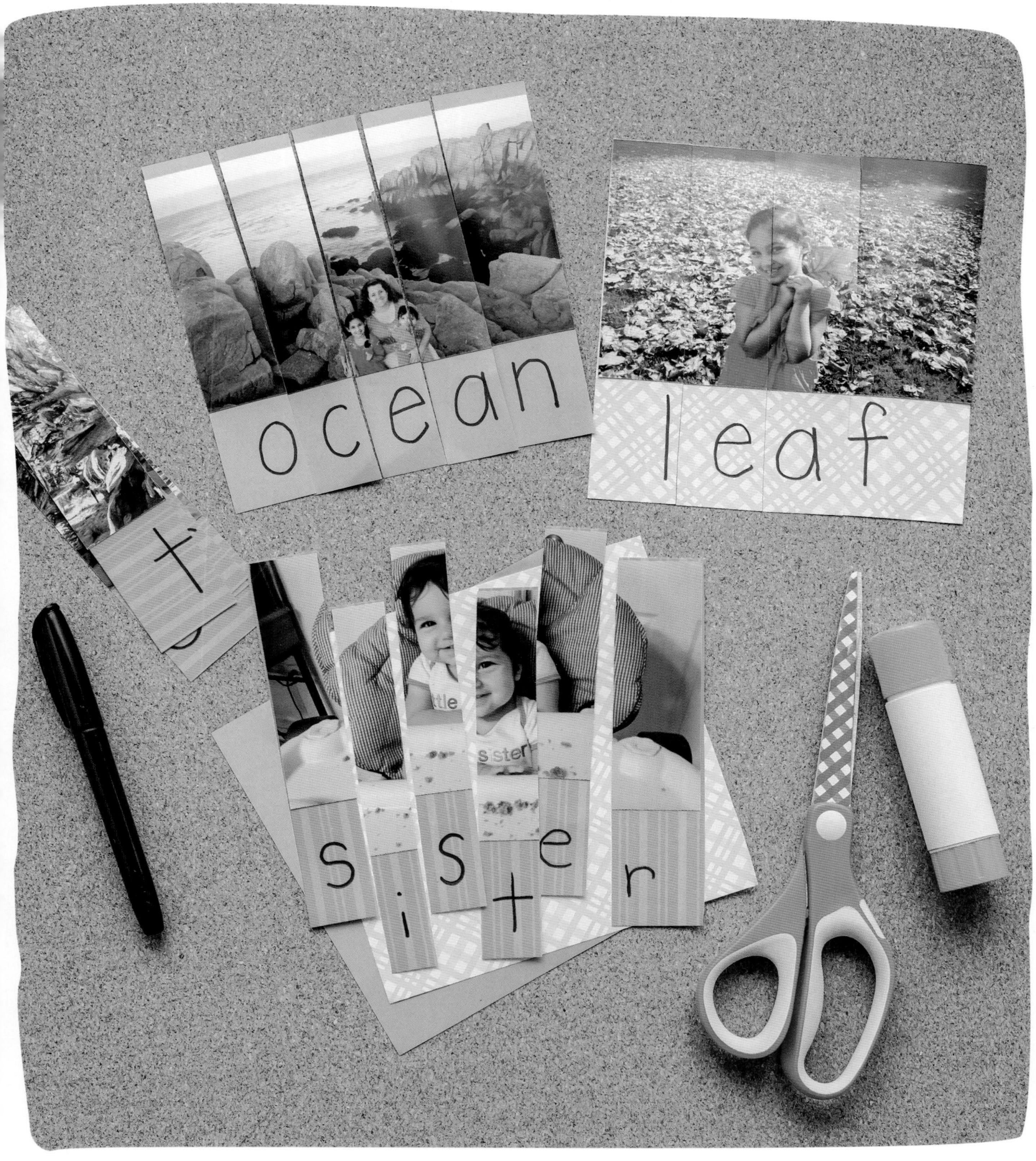

ocean
leaf
sister

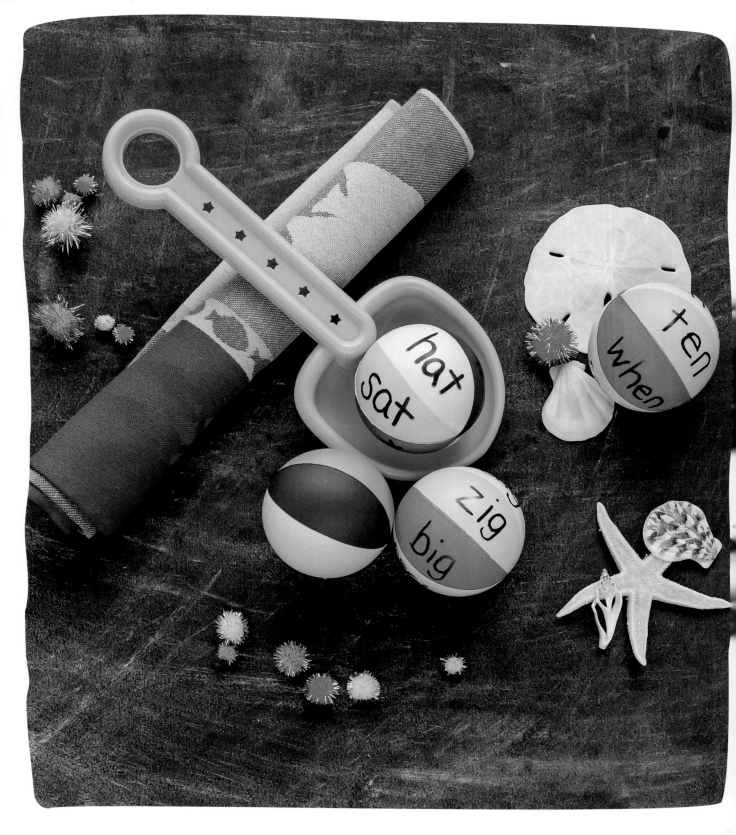

WORD FAMILY TOSS

Word families are words that share a common set of letters that make a similar sound. The "_at" family words are often taught first: cat, hat, bat, mat, rat and sat are all in the "_at" word family. Learning these words helps children gain familiarity with common spelling patterns. Repeated readings of a word help build familiarity and confidence with reading. Using beach balls brings a playful element to reading words and gets kids moving and working together!

Focus Skill: reading words from the same word family endings, rhyming words

Great for: moving while you learn

Materials

3 rainbow-colored beach balls

Permanent marker

Directions to Make

1. Select three word families to focus on, such as "_at," "_en" and "_ig."
2. Write the words from the selected word families on each beach ball color section.

cat, rat, mat, hat, pat, sat

pig, wig, dig, fig, big, zig

pen, men, hen, ten, when, den

Directions to Play

1. In this game, children will gently toss the word family ball to each other. As they catch the ball, they will read the first word they see.
2. If the ball drops, then the child reads all the words on the ball.
3. Play continues for several rounds.
4. Swap out balls as children gain familiarity with reading the words.

Game Variations

★ If children are in a long line, start the ball at the beginning of the line and play pass the word. Players call out the first word they see on the ball as they receive it.

★ For an extra challenge, try throwing and catching two word family balls at a time.

★ Use this game to practice assigned spelling or vocabulary words.

FLUTTERING BUTTERFLIES

Let your word butterflies fly, then catch them as the word ends. Say the last sound you hear, then let them fly again! Playing with words is extremely beneficial for helping children to develop a better ear for sounds. This game is all about listening for those sounds.

 Focus Skill: isolating and pronouncing final sounds

Great For: moving while you learn

Materials

Tissue paper rectangles 2" x 4"
(5 x 10-cm)

Directions to Make

1. Select two tissue paper rectangles. Set them on top of each other and pinch the middles together.

2. Twist at the middle so the two rectangles stay together in a butterfly shape.

Directions to Play

1. Throw a butterfly up in the air.

2. Say a word slowly as the butterfly flutters downward.

3. Catch the butterfly as the word ends.

4. Say the last sound heard in the word.

5. Repeat with another word.

Note

We used our same twisted butterflies for two weeks of word-catching fun and they did not come untwisted! If you wanted to tie a bow in the middle, you could.

Game Variations

★ Try to find the ending sounds in longer words.

★ Encourage your child to think of and say words that end with the same sound.

★ Catch the butterfly on the beginning or middle sound to emphasize different sounds in the word.

PREPOSITION CHARADES

Use your creativity to act out the chosen preposition. Children must know what prepositions are, so that when they come across them in a story they will be able to comprehend what is happening. Pick up any storybook and read for the prepositions. They are there! Then get silly with this pre-reading game that requires a wee bit of acting skills. See if you can get your teammates to correctly guess the word.

 Focus Skill: using and reading the most frequently occurring prepositions

Great For: on-the-go learning

Materials

3″ x 5″ (7.5 x 13-cm) notecards

Scissors

Pencil

Box

Toys

Directions to Make

1. Cut each of the notecards in half.
2. Write one preposition word on each card: in, on, near, under, over, below, above, around, between, behind, in front of, up, down, out, over.

Directions to Play

1. Turn the cards word side down.
2. Have the child read the word and act out the word using the box and toy props.
3. The other players try to guess the preposition using a sentence to describe the preposition.
4. The player who guesses the preposition correctly then draws a new card from the pile.
5. Play continues until all cards have been read and performed.

Game Variations

★ Play this game using a dollhouse and accessories to act out the prepositions.

★ For extra support, have the adult read the word out loud and children work in pairs to act out the preposition.

★ Draw a card, act it out and have the players write their sentence guesses on a piece of paper.

MUFFIN TIN SYLLABLE COUNTING

Say and count syllables in this self-checking muffin tin game. Sneak in a little fine motor practice and boost early literacy skills while picking up buttons. Let the kids help draw the game pieces and you tie in art and creativity too.

Focus Skill: counting syllables in spoken words

Materials

2″ (5-cm) circle

Cardstock

Pencil

Crayons or markers

Scissors

12 cup muffin tin

Buttons

Game Variations

★ Focus the pictures on a specific learning theme such as natural life, ocean or transportation.

★ Select and read a story. Use vocabulary words and characters from the story to make the picture cards.

★ Focus on number sense by changing the pictures to numbers. Have the player count out the buttons to match the written number.

Directions to Make

1. Trace around the 2-inch (5-cm) circle 12 times on the cardstock.

2. Draw a picture of a person, place or thing inside each circle. Cutting pictures from magazines works too! Some examples are dog, caterpillar, fish, bicycle, shoe, car, banana, apple, book, table, circus and library.

3. Color and cut out each picture.

4. Turn the circles over and make a dot for each syllable in the word. The back of the circle with the dog picture would have one dot; caterpillar would have four.

Directions to Play

1. Place the pictures, image side up, in the muffin tin. The player names the picture out loud and counts the number of syllables in the word.

2. The player drops the same number of buttons as syllables in the tin.

3. Play continues until all compartments have been filled with buttons. When this happens, the player self-checks and corrects the number of syllables by turning the picture over and comparing the number of buttons in each compartment with the number of circles on the back of the image.

MAKE iT LONGER

My kids get in the car and start playing this game automatically—it is one of their favorite on-the-go literacy games and is really good for strengthening vocabulary skills. Even the 2-year-old joins in. He likes to be the one who starts the sentences.

For this game, take a simple sentence and add just one describing word to make it longer. Vocabulary is one of the five components to literacy instruction. This game encourages children to really understand the words they are using. A young child may not be able to read the words catch and furry, but they understand what they mean. This game is done orally to really focus on this vocabulary development.

Reviewing describing words prior to playing the game may make it easier for children to come up with ways to make their sentences longer!

 Focus Skill: expanding complete sentences

 Great for: on-the-go learning

Materials

None

Directions to Play

1. One child begins by saying a simple sentence out loud. For example, I see a dog.

2. The next player uses the same words and adds one word or phrase to the sentence. I see a black dog.

3. The players continue to repeat the sentence on their turn and add a word or phrase more on each turn.

I see a black dog run fast.

I see a furry black dog run fast.

I see a furry black dog run fast to catch a mouse.

I see a furry black dog run fast to catch a grey mouse.

I see a furry black dog run fast to catch a little grey mouse.

4. The game stops when the sentence becomes too long to remember!

Game Variations

★ Have advanced learners write their last sentence down on paper.

★ Provide props such as stuffed animals for children to act out the sentence, which aids in memory.

★ Encourage the use of specific spelling or vocabulary words in the sentences.

STORYTELLING PUZZLES

Characters in stories draw our children's attention. Using handmade puzzles that you create together, players learn to discuss and compare the various types of characters. Story time discussions about characters enhance reading comprehension and vocabulary development.

Focus Skill: comparing characters in a story

Great For: on-the-go learning

Materials

Favorite storybook

Images from selected story

Paper

Scanner/printer

Scissors

Plastic bag

Directions to Make

1. Create images from favorite parts of a story by drawing or using a scanner to copy and print.
2. Cut each image into 4 to 6 puzzle pieces.

Directions to Play

1. Player selects pieces from the bag in correct order to form images from the story.
2. Encourage players to identify the characters and setting in the story with each image formed.

Game Variations

★ Players can place images in sequence from the story.

★ Players sort completed puzzles into groups of similarities based on characters and setting.

★ Create a magnetic game by placing magnetic stripes on the back of puzzle pieces.

REAL OR NONSENSE?

Make up silly words (and real ones too) by rolling homemade letter dice. Grab a cubed tissue box, cover with paper and add a few letters. Then let your kids roll, read and call out the new word—is it real or nonsense? My kids have added their own "spin" to the game and make a silly face when the word rolled doesn't make sense. Bat, get, fan and men are all real words, but gip is a nonsense word!

Focus Skill: blending together sounds to make simple words

Materials

Paper

Scissors

3 square tissue boxes

Tape or glue

Black marker

Directions to Make

1. Cut 18 squares of paper to cover each side of the tissue boxes. Tape or glue the paper to the boxes.
2. Write consonants on the sides of two boxes and vowels on the third box.

> Dice 1: b, c, f, p, r, m
>
> Dice 2: t, d, g, h, l, n
>
> Dice 3: a, e, i, o, u, a

Directions to Play

1. Roll the three dice.
2. Arrange them in order so the vowel is in the middle.
3. Say the sounds for each letter. Blend the sounds together to say the word.
4. Shout the word out. Is it real or nonsense?

Game Variations

★ For long vowel words, add in an extra vowel dice.

★ To practice the long vowel with a silent e words, add in an extra dice with all e's.

★ To work on words with just one vowel sound, use only one letter for the vowel die.

SIGHT WORD SENSORY BOTTLE

Add a little sparkle and bedazzle to your literacy learning with some shiny beads and sequins. Make a few of these sight word sensory bottles to use throughout the year. Set them out on a small table near your bookshelves for an interactive sight word experience. Look for different colors, textures and words. Listen to the sounds the fillers make as you shake the bottle to find all the sight words in this sensory bottle game. Rotate the bottles as your child has demonstrated mastery of the selected words.

Focus Skill: sight word recognition, fluency

Materials

Empty, clean 2-liter soda bottle

Tiny filler items such as rice, beads, sequins or bells

Small foam rectangles

Black permanent marker

One-minute sand timer

Directions to Make

1. Fill the bottle halfway with tiny fillers of your choosing.
2. Write five chosen sight words on the foam rectangles. Sample sight words: I, the, and, see, it.
3. Add the words to the bottle.
4. Close the lid tightly and shake until the words and fillers mix.

Directions to Play

1. Set the timer for 1 minute.
2. Roll the bottle and read.
3. See if you can find all five words before the time ends.

Note

Sight words are common words in the English language that your child will encounter throughout his or her life. Learning to recognize and read these words quickly will help with reading fluency. Some of these words cannot be sounded out and must be memorized through games and repeated exposure.

Game Variations

★ Dump the contents of the bottle into a plastic bin to create a sensory play experience.

★ Fill the bottle with words from a specific word family for decoding practice.

★ Use letter beads instead of words. Have the child search for the letters in alphabetical order!

SIGHT WORD GEMS

Learning to read becomes quite magical with these sight word gems. Players quickly search to find the match, which helps them build fluency with sight word recognition. A child's ability to quickly recognize sight words helps them to become successful readers. You can put your sight word gems in a plastic bag for on-the-go fun at restaurants.

Focus Skill: identfying sight words with fluency

Great for: on-the-go learning

Materials

Glass gems

Permanent black marker

Scrapbook or construction paper

List of basic sight words

Small container

Directions to Make

1. Write the selected sight words onto the glass gems with the permanent marker and allow to dry. Use words (like one, my, the, to, you) that cannot be traditionally sounded out like consonant-vowel-consonant (CVC) words.

2. Write the same words onto a colorful sheet of paper, ensuring that they are easily read.

Directions to Play

1. Place the sight word sheet on a flat surface.

2. Read the sight words out loud with the players.

3. Ask each player to select a sight word gem and find the match.

4. When the player places the sight word gem onto the match, encourage them to identify the word.

5. Continue until all of the words have been used.

Game Variations

★ Create sight word matches for players to find the match in a memory game.

★ Play sight word scavenger hunt using gems around the room.

★ Write the letters on the glass gems and have each player create the sight word listed on the paper.

AMAZING WRITING ADVENTURES

Playing writing games with children is an easy way to make writing fun and promote reading. Children develop reading skills such as decoding new words alongside their writing skills. Often, a child's writing skills will clue adults in on the writer's understanding of letters and words.

Younger writers begin with scribbles on a page and move toward the formation of objects and eventually letters, words, sentences and stories. Adults can help support this growth and development by providing opportunities for children to write.

Use big blank white sheets of paper to start with and a variety of writing materials. Pens, markers and crayons are all great instruments for young learners. Encourage creative exploration with writing strokes. As the child shows an interest in letters, encourage them to listen for and write the sounds in words. Correct spelling comes with an increased understanding in patterns of words.

COMMUNITY CORNER

What is your best tip for getting kids excited about writing?

"Giving them opportunities and activities that they will want to write out! My son was told that writers gather topics they will write about later as they live each day."

—Deirdre S.

"Fun tools! Great pencils, smelly markers, colored pencils. Young writers can practice writing in sand, on dry erase boards and those magnetic pen boards. My own kids said they also like an incentive to get them to write: an author celebration or a prize."

—Kristen M.

"My daughter is just learning to write words and sound them out. Her sense of accomplishment and pride each time she does it just fills me with joy! Her favorite activity is writing secret or surprise messages for people."

—Laura D.

"Oftentimes writers are frustrated because they do not have someone to write TO. Kids need an audience. A reader. Someone who will respond to their creation, ask questions or comment. Give them feedback. That audience or reader can make writing more authentic and much more meaningful to young writers."

—Becky S.

"Giving children the space and time to discover language—reading and writing—on their own. There is a range of development. Step back and watch it unfold with the child as the leader."

—Marnie C.

"Providing kids with authentic, relevant reasons to write is a surefire way to get them excited about writing! Encourage children to write a letter to a favorite author, support them as they write toy or book reviews or help them set up their own blog or website, and the possibilities for meaningful writing are endless."

—Amy M.

"Invite children to write about things they love most. If action figurines are their thing, help them brainstorm exciting superhero adventures. If they're into princesses, make a list of princess story topics."

—Malia H.

WORDS IN THE SAND

Find hidden words on seashells in the sand to encourage your child to learn to read. Players quickly memorize each word by writing it into the sand in a texture-rich experience. This multi-sensory game helps to engage children's senses as they learn their sight words.

Focus Skill: identifying and writing sight words

Materials

Permanent black marker

Seashells

Sand

2 plastic containers or trays

Directions to Make

1. Write sight words onto seashells.
2. Place the seashells in one container.
3. Place sand in the second container or tray.

Directions to Play

1. Players take turns pulling seashells from the container.
2. Once they've selected them, players identify the word and write it in the sand container.
3. Continue to play until all the word seashells are discovered and written in the sand.

Game Variations

★ Create letters in the sand for younger players to discover and write.

★ Form words from letter shells in the sand and write them in the sand container.

★ Write numbers on the shells for players to discover and write.

MAKE A WORD

Phonics is a big part of early literacy. This make-a-word game provides opportunities for children to apply their knowledge of letters and sounds to build words in a fun way, then connect them to the written word.

Focus Skill: spelling three-letter words with two consonants and one vowel in the middle

Materials

5 (3" x 5" [7.5 x 13-cm]) notecards

Scissors

Black and red markers

Dice

Paper

Pencil

Directions to Make

1. Cut each of the notecards in half.

2. Write one letter on each card. Make sure to use two vowels and eight consonants total. It is optional to write the vowels in red. Sample set of letters: a, e, c, m, t, p, r, b, h, n.

Directions to Play

1. Turn the cards letter side down.

2. Roll the dice. Say the number rolled out loud.

3. Count out that many letter cards.

4. Make a word with the selected letters.

5. Write that word on a piece of paper.

6. Continue making new words with the selected cards. When no more words can be made, count the total number of words made. There is a three-minute time limit to each turn.

7. Turn the cards upside down and pass the dice to the next player.

8. After three rounds, total the number of words written. The player with the most wins the game!

Game Variations

★ For beginning readers, use only one vowel card. Keep that card face up and roll for the consonants.

★ Encourage the players to select three words to write sentences with at the end of each game.

★ Turn all the cards over and work together to make a list of all the possible words that could be made with the selected letters.

GUESS MY FAVORITE

Writing about favorite books and toys is a great way to make writing meaningful to your child. The added guessing creates anticipation and excitement for literacy! This writing game is adaptable to all skill levels. Children can draw, write words or use sentences depending on their writing ability. With early writers, an adult can write the words the child wants to say next to the picture.

Focus Skill: composing an opinion

Materials

Half sheets of cardstock

Writing materials

Directions to Play

1. Select a favorite book or toy from the shelves. Do NOT tell the other players what it is.

2. Write down information about the toy or book and why it is your favorite.

Sample:

It's a book.

It has a cute caterpillar on it.

It is a fun book with holes on each page.

I like to count the fruit.

What book is it?

3. Read the clues out loud. Let the other players guess what book it is.

4. Repeat steps 1 through 3 with another favorite book or toy.

Game Variations

★ Set out a group of five fruits and play the game with only these items.

★ Have two children choose the same object and write their opinions about it. Compare.

★ Encourage advanced learners to create a set of clue cards and staple them together to make a Guess My Favorites homemade book.

YOU DRAW, I DRAW, LET'S MAKE A SENTENCE

Unleash your inner artist with this partner drawing and writing game. Use your imagination and creativity to turn a rock into an ice cream cone. Each silly little doodle will inspire a sentence. This game also challenges children to expand their vocabulary skills. What to write about will not be a problem for children since they have drawn pictures throughout the game, activating the words in their mind. Having an adult write the sentence helps young children make the connection between oral and written language.

Focus Skill: producing a complete sentence

Materials

Printer paper

Pencil

Crayons (optional)

Directions to Make

1. Talk about what makes a sentence. Each sentence must have a subject. A subject is who or what the sentence is about. A sentence also has a verb, or action word that tells what the subject is doing. "The train chugs along the tracks." In this sentence, the train is the subject and chugs is the verb.

Directions to Play

1. One player doodles a quick simple object on the piece of paper. They pass the picture to the next player.

2. The second player adds on to the object or draws another one next to the first.

3. The two players then create a sentence orally to describe their picture. An adult writes the sentence on the paper.

4. Repeat steps 1 through 3 until the paper is filled with pictures and sentences.

Game Variations

★ Encourage advanced learners to write the sentences on their own.

★ Play the game in a large group. Each person begins with a piece of paper. They draw an object and pass the paper to the player on the right. They then draw on the paper in front of them. Play continues until each player has drawn something on each paper. When the paper returns to the original owner, the player makes up a sentence for their picture.

★ Focus on writing words by having the players label the objects with words instead of making a sentence.

SHOP THE ALPHABET

Going to the grocery store with your child can be a great learning experience. When you're armed with a clipboard, paper and pencil, your next shopping trip will be a breeze. Can you find a food for every letter of the alphabet?

Focus Skill: writing a list

Materials

Clipboard

Paper

Pencil

Directions to Make

1. Clip a piece of paper on the clipboard.

2. Write the letters of the alphabet on the left-hand side of the page.

Directions to Play

1. Take the clipboard to the grocery store. Each player may have his or her own game board or work together to complete one. Name a food item that you see. Say the beginning sound, and then write the word next to that letter on the page. For example, A: apple. B: banana. C: carrots. Inventive and phonetic spelling is encouraged for young learners.

2. Each letter may be used only one time. Find one food item that begins with each letter before you reach the checkout counter.

Game Variations

★ For younger learners, the child may identify the food and beginning sound and the adult writes the word for the child to trace.

★ Select only four letters and make a list of everything found beginning with those sounds.

★ For advanced learners, challenge them to take the grocery list and alphabetize it.

SNEAK-A-PEEK LETTERS

What begins with B? Let's sneak-a-peek for a clue in this super cute kid-made writing game. Young children gravitate toward being able to cut pictures out of magazines. Turn this fun craft activity into a writing game that focuses on the beginning letters of words.

Focus Skill: writing beginning sounds in words

Materials

Paper

Scissors

Kid-friendly magazines

Glue

Directions to Make

1. Fold the paper in half the long way.
2. Cut three slits evenly spaced apart on one half of the sheet.

Directions to Play

1. Find a picture in the magazine. Cut it out and glue it under a flap.
2. Say the name of the picture. Figure out the beginning sound. Write the letter for that sound on the top of the flap.
3. Repeat until the top three flaps are filled with letters and the spaces below are filled with pictures.
4 Hand the game board to another child. They will say the sound the letter makes and try to guess the word that begins with that sound. If they need a clue, they can sneak-a-peek.
5. Repeat for all three letters.

Game Variations

★ Write the word on the top. Lift the flap for a self-checking reading game.

★ Encourage children to write a full sentence clue on the top flap.

★ Write a story with a beginning, middle and end on each flap. Use pictures from a magazine to illustrate each section under the words.

BUILD A WORD

Words come to life for players as they build their first words using handmade alphabet blocks. Players use items from their play area or familiar places and items to begin to learn how to spell them out. This game gives players the chance to practice in a bigger way as they start to form words from left to right with the blocks and then again on paper.

 Focus Skill: learning how to write words from left to right

Materials

Cardboard or tagboard

Scissors

Tape

Black marker

Alphabet stickers (optional)

Packaging tape (optional)

Construction paper or scrapbook paper

Directions to Make

1. Use the cardboard to create a box for dice by cutting it into a lowercase "t" shape. Repeat to make 6 in all.

2. Fold the sides for a box and tape together.

3. Write letters of the alphabet onto the blocks. Alphabet stickers or store-bought alphabet blocks can be used as an alternative.

4. Cover the blocks with packaging tape for durability if you'd like.

5. Select everyday items from around the house, pets and family members for words to use with game.

6. Write the words for the items onto the paper with your child to make the word sheet.

7. On a separate sheet of paper, copy or draw images and make a blank line for the word.

Directions to Play

1. Select a word from the word sheet.

2. Using the ABC blocks, build the word.

3. Use the word sheet to check your spelling.

4. Once correct, write down the word that you created next to the picture on the paper.

Game Variations

★ Create word families with the ABC blocks.

★ Write down letters on a sheet of poster board and encourage players to place blocks onto matching letters.

★ Stack ABC letters with similarities, such as curves, slants and straight lines.

MYSTERY WORDS

Grab some glue and paper and head to the sandbox for this crafty writing game that even sneaks in some fine motor strengthening. Make sure to have a few extra pieces of paper available for children to keep sand writing.

Focus Skill: writing words

Materials

Glue

Half sheets of paper or cardstock

Sand

Directions to Play

1. Choose a word in your mind, but don't say it out loud. Glue the shape of the beginning letter on the piece of paper. Sprinkle sand over the glue and gently shake off. Ask the player to your right to guess your word based on that first letter. They will have three guesses. If they have guessed correctly, it is their turn to start glue writing a different word.

2. If the first three guesses are not correct, then player one adds another glue letter to the word, sprinkles sand over the glue and gently shakes the sand off. The player to the right has three more guesses.

3. Play continues until the word has been identified.

4. Repeat steps 1 through 3 so each child playing the game has the opportunity to build at least two words.

5. Let the words dry.

6. Staple the paper together to make a sandy word book!

Game Variations

★ Write the child's name with the sand.

★ Write your school spelling words.

★ Make five sets of rhyming words and play a matching game.

ALL iN MY HOUSE

Kids easily create their own sentences inspired by their home environment. Using word sticks, kids will form sentences from left to right with confidence. Selecting from predetermined words gives them more chances to create several sentences at writing time.

Focus Skill: creating a sentence with words

Materials

30 to 50 Popsicle sticks

Black marker

Container

Paper

Directions to Make

1. Create a list of words with your child about parts of their home.
    a. Create a list of things in their home.
    b. Create a list of people in their home.
    c. Create a list of actions at home.
2. Write the selected words onto Popsicle sticks.
3. Sort the words into four piles with person, place, action and thing.
4. Write on sticks basic sight words—such as too, like, my, is, the, on, at, can, I, see—for each player to keep with them at all times by their house.
5. Create a house outline using extra Popsicle sticks to place word sticks into.

Directions to Play

1. Ask players to choose Popsicle sticks from all four categories: person, place, action and thing.
2. Then encourage them to create a sentence using those sticks (example: The cat is sleeping in the bedroom, Mom is cooking in the kitchen) and any of the sight word sticks.
3. Place the completed sentence into the Popsicle house.

Game Variations

★ Players can sort Popsicle stick words by nouns and verbs.

★ Players can write completed sentences onto a sheet of paper.

★ Players can form houses with the word sticks in proper sentence order.

WRITE ON

This writing game works well in small groups of kids who have mastered writing sentences. It provides children with a way to practice their creative writing skills in a fun game that results in a shared story.

Just one adult and child? No problem. This game can be played with just two players as well! What are you waiting for? Grab a pencil and start writing!

Focus Skill: participating in shared writing projects

Materials

Lined paper for each player

Pencil

Timer

Directions to Play

1. Every child begins the game with one piece of paper. The time starts and each child begins to write a story.

2. The parent or teacher keeps time. After 4 minutes, everyone stops and passes their story to the right. The timekeeper waits for everyone to receive their new papers and says, "Write on."

3. Children read what has been written on the page and continue writing the story.

4. Repeat steps 2 and 3 for a minimum of three more rounds. Return the story to its original writer.

5. Allow the children time to write the story ending if it has not already been done.

6. Read the stories out loud.

Game Variations

★ For younger children, play this writing game with pictures. Use three boxes. Each player will tell the beginning, middle or ending of the story with their drawings.

★ Have an adult write down the child's story and let them trace or fill in some key words.

★ Use a large piece of paper. Have children alternate telling the story while the adult writes down the words.

STORYTELLING SEASHELLS

Spin a tale with these cute kid-made storytelling seashells. Collect some shells while you are on a beach vacation or purchase them at your local craft store. Paint characters and places from their favorite stories inside each shell. Turn them over and select a few to weave your own tale and write your story!

Focus Skill: writing a story

Materials

Clean shells

Newspaper

Acrylic paints

Plastic lid

Paintbrush

Paper

Pencil

Directions to Make

1. Set the clean shells inside up on the newspaper.

2. Pour a small amount of paint onto a plastic lid. Set near the shells.

3. Encourage your child to paint small pictures of characters and places/settings from the fairy tales they know inside the shells. Examples: mermaid—ocean, king—castle, boy in blue—haystack, mouse—clock.

4. Allow the shells to dry.

Directions to Play

1. Place the character shells face down in one pile and the setting shells face down in another pile.

2. Select one character and one setting shell.

3. Use the selected shells as the beginning of the story. Add a preposition word (inside, behind, on, next to) to make the title.

4. Write the story down on paper.

Game Variations

★ Play this game as an oral storytelling activity.

★ Short on time? Encourage children to write one sentence rather than the whole story.

★ Perform the story for an audience.

REALLY COOL MATH

Developing a solid foundation in mathematics is vital to a child's future success in school. It is important for children to know how to count and recognize numbers, but also to grasp what those numbers represent and be able to manipulate them to solve problems. The best way to strengthen these academic concepts is through repetition of hands-on, playful learning.

Math manipulatives can be made out of store-bought supplies, household materials and natural found objects. A traditional early childhood classroom will most likely have blocks, colored counters, a scale and analog clocks. Recyclables such as bottle lids, paper tubes, corks and containers are also useful. Sticks, stones, leaves and flowers from the natural environment can all be counted, sorted and used in math games as well.

There are many ways you can help get and keep your child excited about math. Point out the many times when you use math throughout your day. Play store-bought board games and homemade games, too. Smile when you talk about numbers. Celebrate when your child masters a mathematics skill.

COMMUNITY CORNER

How do you get your child excited about math?

"I get my daughter excited by talking about how math is used in real life and stressing that practically every job out there requires math skills. She also sees me using math for my work, especially graphs and percentages."

—Natalie F.

"I get my 4-year-old son excited about math through hands-on materials that allow him to explore mathematical concepts long before he is able to define them. He can make a rectangle using two triangles or count using rocks or other nature items; simple times for engaging mathematical play teaches him that math is useful and fun."

—Amy S.

"I use projects, rather than worksheets, and it gets him excited. I also use cooking a lot, and sports, now that he plays hockey, and he says math is his favorite subject."

—Laurie F.

"My kids have been introduced to early-math concepts (colors, shapes, counting) through books and daily conversation. We read books every day, and while I sometimes get specific books from the library, our reading is usually driven by my kids' choices. My 3-year-old has had periods where he's interested in letters or numbers and he tends to pick books that relate. During those times, I try to make some activities/materials available to him that relate (things like sorting activities, magnetic letters, shape sorters). He's pretty big on driving his own play, though, so I don't push lots of directed activities. Rather, it's just providing materials that allow him to pursue his interests. For us, it's really about learning through play."

—Kathleen S.

"I've always felt that you think math, you don't 'do' math. Letting your kids keep a pair of dice or a deck of cards in their pocket and playing with them often can introduce and develop a love of math and numbers!"

—Glenyce P.

"My 8-year-old is very visual and kinesthetic... she gets excited about math when it includes three-dimensional manipulatives (and bonus points if they're cute)!"

—Carla J.

NUMBER HOOPS

Players have fun shouting out their answer and throwing it through the Hula-Hoop to help learn their math facts. Using balls with the answers, players solve given number sentences like 4 + 2 = _ and quickly grab the answer and throw the number 6 through the target. Making this a math game with movement will help them use more senses as they learn.

 Focus Skill: solving number sentences

Great For: moving while you learn

Materials

Paper

Black marker

Scissors

Hula-Hoop

Tape

11 balls

Directions to Make

1. Write number sentences on paper. Select ones that equal no more than 10. For example: 4 + 1 = ___ or 2 + 2 = ___.
2. Cut them into cards for players to choose from.
3. Hang up a Hula-Hoop so that players can toss balls through it.
4. Write numbers 0 to 10 on paper and cut into cards for answers.
5. With tape, attach the number answers to the balls from 0 to 10.

Directions to Play

1. Player selects a number sentence to solve.
2. Player solves the problem by finding the ball with the correct answer and throwing the numbered ball through the hanging Hula-Hoop.
3. Each player continues until all the number sentences have been selected.

Game Variations

★ Hang up multiple Hula-Hoops and have players select which number to throw the ball through based on the answer to the number sentence.

★ Have players throw number balls through the Hula-Hoop in numerical order.

★ Have players toss numbered balls in skip counting order through the Hula-Hoop.

BUILD A NUMBER PUZZLE

Discover how quickly you can put together a number! Challenge your friend to see who is the fastest in building numbers. Learning the shapes of numbers can help children learn to write and recognize them more easily.

focus Skill: recognizing numbers

Great for: on-the-go learning

Materials

Black marker

Construction paper

Scissors

Contact paper or packing tape (optional)

Directions to Make

1. Draw a large outline of numbers 0 to 10 onto various colors of paper.
2. Cut out the numbers.
3. Cover the numbers with contact paper for durability, if you'd like.
4. Cut each number into three pieces to create puzzle pieces.

Directions to Play

1. Arrange the number puzzle pieces on a flat surface.
2. Each player selects a piece when it is their turn and begins to form a number.
3. Players take turns drawing number pieces strategically to form the most numbers.
4. The game ends when all of the pieces have been drawn.
5. The winner is the one with the most completed number puzzles!

Game Variations

★ For added difficulty, keep the number puzzle pieces in a bag or have players close their eyes when selecting, so they cannot see the pieces they are drawing.

★ Cut the number shapes into more or fewer pieces or race to see who builds the quickest.

★ Use the child's own recycled artwork to form the paper pieces.

BEAD iT!

Beads come in all sorts of shapes and colors. Children love to thread them onto strings and craft wires. Not only is this great for fine motor practice, but it's also a springboard into early mathematics. In this game, children will race the clock to bead numbers 1 to 9. Store this game in a Ziplock bag and tuck it into your purse for on-the-go learning.

 Focus Skill: representing numbers 0 to 9

Great for: on-the-go learning

Materials

5 craft wires

Scissors

Small paper rectangles, 1″ x 2″ (2.5 x 5 cm)

Tape

Permanent marker

Sand timer

Pony beads

Directions to Make

1. Cut each craft wire in half.

2. Tape one side of the paper rectangle to the bottom of the craft wire and fold over to form a square. Repeat for nine craft wires total.

3. Write the numbers 1 to 9 on the squares.

Directions to Play

1. Turn the sand timer over.

2. Bead the same number of beads on each wire as written on the paper square.

3. Shape the wire into the shape of the number.

4. Try to build as many numbers as possible before the timer runs out.

Game Variations

★ Build and put the numbers in order from the least to the greatest.

★ Use a specific pattern when beading the numbers.

★ Call out a number and have the child build the beads for the numbers that equal that sum. If "10" is called, the child could build the 4 and 6 craft wires.

25 SQUISH

$$3 + 1 = 4$$
$$4 + 3 = 7$$
$$7 + 6 = 13$$
$$13 + \underline{} = \underline{}$$
$$\underline{} + \underline{} = \underline{}$$
$$\underline{} + \underline{} = \underline{}$$

25 SQUISH

Connect fine motor strengthening and mathematics with this hands-on play dough squishing game! Children will roll spheres to match the numbers they roll, then count and add the sum. The next player adds more spheres to the pile until the total reaches 25 or more. Then they get to SQUISH them! This game provides children with much needed concrete math practice with numbers up to 25.

Focus Skill: addition to 25

Materials

Yarn

Pencil

Paper

Die

Play dough

Game Variations

★ Start with 25 spheres. Smash on each turn for a simple subtraction game.

★ For an added challenge— bump the final number up to 50 or 100!

★ No play dough? Use dot markers and have players add a dot for the numbers rolled onto a large sheet of paper.

Directions to Make

1. Use the yarn to make a large circle on the table. This will signify the workspace for the child. All play dough spheres will be placed inside this circle.

2. Write the words 25 SQUISH on the top of the paper.

3. Directly under the words, make six rows for addition number sentences under the title. Each line will look like this ____ + ____ = ____.

Directions to Play

1. For the first round: Roll the die. Count and write the number rolled on the recording sheet in the first space. Roll the same number of play dough spheres and put them in the yarn circle. Roll the die again. Count and write the number in the second space on the recording sheet. Make the same number of play dough spheres and add them to the yarn circle. Count the total and write the total on the recording sheet in the last blank.

2. Pass the die, paper and pencil to the next player.

3. The next player will count the number of spheres in the circle. They will write this number in the first blank of the next number sentence. They will then roll the die one time and write that number in the second blank. The child will make that many more spheres and add them to the yarn circle. When the play dough spheres have been added to the yarn circle, the child must count and find out how many spheres are in the circle. This is finding the sum or total amount. This total number is written on the third blank space in the number sentence.

4. Pass the die and repeat step 3 until there are 25 or more spheres in the yarn circle.

5. The player who makes 25 or more gets to squish each sphere.

3, 2, 1 BLAST OFF!

Challenge your child to install the rocket ship windows in the correct number order before blasting off into space. Players attach windows onto the spaceship to practice their number skills in a playful way.

Focus Skill: recognizing numbers and number order

Materials

Rocket ship outline

Black marker

Poster board

10 small white circles

Clothespins

Tape

Directions to Make

1. Draw and color a rocket ship with your child on the poster board.
2. On the rocket, write numbers 1 to 10 for each window, to be clipped on in order from top to bottom.
3. Write the numbers 1 to 10 on the white circles for windows.
4. Attach the numbered white circles for the windows onto each clothespin with tape.

Directions to Play

1. Players take turns selecting numbered window clothespins from the pile and attaching to the correct number on the rocket ship.
2. Game continues until all of the rocket ship windows are installed.
3. Once filled, countdown to BLAST OFF!

Game Variations

★ For advanced children use numbers 1 to 20.

★ Write number sentences on the windows and have them solve them by placing the correct number on the rocket ship.

★ Focus on skip counting by counting by tens, fives or twos with the numbers on the rocket ship and windows.

SUNSHINE NUMBERS

Shine a little math into your day with this crafty clothespin number-matching game. Children will delight in adding the rays to the paper plate sun over and over again. They will have repeated exposure to how many dots each number represents. This will help them develop a deeper understanding of what each number is. Repetition helps strengthen a child's understanding of any given academic concept.

Focus Skill: representing a given number of dots with the numeral

Materials

Paper plate

Markers

Yellow paper

Scissors

Glue

16 clothespins

Directions to Make

1. Have your child decorate the paper plate with the marker.
2. Cut out thin rectangles from the yellow paper. These will be the sun's rays.
3. Glue one rectangle to each clothespin.
4. Write the numbers 0 to 15 on the outside edge of the paper plate.
5. Make small dots on each yellow rectangle equal to the numbers 0 to 15.

Directions to Play

1. Count the number of dots on the sun ray.
2. Match the ray to the written number on the paper plate. Clip on top.
3. Repeat with the remaining clothespins until you have a full shining sun!

Game Variations

★ For younger children, match the number with the number.

★ For advanced learners, write number sentences on the sun rays. Put the answers on the edge of the paper plate.

★ Use two color rays, yellow and orange. Have children make and extend a pattern.

HOW MANY BRICKS

Finding math in everyday moments encourages your child to learn to group items by specific numbers. This is the perfect game for playtime, snack time or on-the-go. Children begin to build confidence in their ability to count as they explore numbers.

Focus Skill: sorting and grouping items into specific number grouping

Materials

Black marker

Paper

Scissors

Plastic bricks or any small item

Container

10 muffin tin liners, plastic or paper

Directions to Make

1. Write the numbers 0 to 10 on paper and cut them out into number cards.
2. Collect a pile of plastic bricks or any small toy, or even snack items, to count.
3. Place the small items into a container.
4. Place the number cards next to the container with items.
5. Each player lines up the muffin liners to start playing.

Directions to Play

1. Player selects a number card and orally counts the plastic bricks and places them into a muffin liner.
2. Players take turns until they have filled all of their muffin liners, matching the numbers with the correct number of items.

Game Variations

★ Players can connect each plastic brick on top of one another to add up to the chosen number.

★ Play game with snack items such as small crackers, popcorn or fruit pieces.

★ For advanced players, have them create number sentences to solve before selecting the number they collect from the container.

MONSTER PLAY DOUGH MATH

Make math memorable with a monster bash! Using googly eyes and your child's imagination, learning to recognize numbers can be a hands-on experience. Learning to group items into set number groups is an important beginning math skill.

Focus Skill: recognizing numbers

Materials

Black marker

Paper

Scissors

Plastic numbers (optional)

Googly eyes

Play dough

Small container

Directions to Make

1. Use the marker and paper to make number cards from 0 to 10. Cut them into cards or use plastic numbers instead.

Directions to Play

1. Give each player googly eyes in a small container and play dough.

2. As players take their turn, they select a number from the pile and create a monster with eyes to match the number drawn.

3. Encourage each player to create monsters with eyes from 0 to 10.

Game Variations

★ Each player can create monsters with a specific number of arms instead of eyes.

★ For advanced players, challenge them with math facts and use eyes to show the answer.

★ Create multiple monsters to match the number drawn.

STAMP YOUR WAY TO THE FINISH!

Have you ever made your own board game before? If you have a paper and pencil and can draw circles, then it's super easy to make. Make one for yourself or a friend to play. Better yet—make a bunch and trade them with friends. Then count and stamp your way to the finish!

Focus Skill: counting forward, beginning from a given number within the known sequence

Materials

Paper

Pencil

Self-inking stamps

Dice

Directions to Make

1. Take a piece of paper and draw a ton of small circles in a line. The line of circles can curve around the paper. The more circles the better.

2. Write the word START at the beginning of your line of circles. Write END after the last circle.

Directions to Play

1. Put your self-inking stamper on the start. For more than one player, use different color stamps.

2. Roll the dice and stamp that number of circles. Say the numbers as they are stamped.

3. Pass the dice to the next player. Roll and stamp.

4. The stamp that reaches the end first wins the game!

Game Variations

★ Write in bonus circles: Land on this circle and roll again.

★ Use a 100 chart as a game board.

★ Switch stamps for coins so that your game board can be reused.

ROCK NUMBER HUNT

Kids discover that numbers rock by being challenged to discover them in their own environment and create their own number groups. Players go on a treasure hunt to discover where the numbers are hiding.

Focus Skill: recognizing numbers

Great For: moving while you learn

Materials

22 rocks

Paint

Paintbrush

Container for each player

Directions to Make

1. Paint numbers onto the rocks with your child and allow to dry.
2. On the other side of the rocks paint shapes to total 10 circles, 6 squares and 6 triangles.
3. Allow time for the paint on the rocks to dry.
4. Hide the rocks.

Directions to Play

1. Players go on a scavenger hunt to collect the number rocks.
2. As players discover the rocks, encourage them to identify the number they find.
3. Players collect number rocks in their container.
4. Once all the number rocks are found, players will practice counting using the other side of the rocks for counters.
5. Players will form a group of rocks to match the selected number.

Game Variations

★ Use rocks to play a shape hunt game.

★ Use rocks to create a shape pattern.

★ Place rocks in numerical order from 0 to 10.

BUTTERFLY SYMMETRY

The mystery of symmetry becomes more interesting when one of your senses is challenged with symmetrical wing design. Players use shapes to create butterfly wings that match by following oral directions. Focusing on symmetry helps a child to develop basic skills of geometry at an early age.

Focus Skill: using listening skills to re-create images using shapes

Materials

Poster board

Markers or paint

Scissors

Blindfold

Directions to Make

1. Create a large butterfly outline from the poster board.
2. Design matching shapes for decorating the wings.

Directions to Play

1. Place the butterfly down on a flat surface to start the game.
2. Set out the shapes to decorate each wing.
3. One player puts on a blindfold while the other describes where to place the pieces to design the butterfly wings.
4. Then the player describes to the blindfolded player where to place which shape to create the same design on the other wing to create symmetry.
5. Switch turns and try again.

Game Variations

★ Create two butterflies and race to see who can create a symmetrical butterfly first.
★ Create puzzle wings that only work in a specific way.
★ Hang the butterfly on the wall and have players attempt to design symmetrical wings blindfolded.

SCOOP 10

Have you ever grabbed a handful of something and "known" how many there were just by glancing at the objects in your hand? This math skill involves special reasoning and number sense. It is also a great way to strengthen your child's understanding of math vocabulary terms: more than, less than and equal to. Join in the game too. See if you can scoop 10!

Focus Skill: counting and recognizing numbers 0 to 20

Materials

Plastic bowl

Pennies (or buttons of the same size)

2 pieces of paper

Pencil

Directions to Make

1. Fill the bowl with pennies.

2. Count and set 10 pennies on a piece of paper next to the game as a visual reference of what 10 pennies look like.

3. On the second sheet of paper, write the names of the players across the top.

Directions to Play

1. Player one reaches into the bowl and grabs a handful of pennies.

2. They open their hand and makes an immediate guess out loud: less than, more than or equal to 10 pennies.

3. The same player then counts the coins. If their guess was correct, they write a point down.

4. The next player scoops, guesses and counts. Play continues until a player reaches five total points.

Game Variations

★ Scoop for five.

★ Use small objects of varying sizes, such as small building bricks, for an extra challenge.

★ Let each child keep the coins they scooped for three turns. Then have them add the total number of coins.

SUPERHERO ZOOM

Zip and zap your way to 100 in this active backyard game that connects math, movement and outside play in a meaningful way. Run from one hero shield to the next as you count by 10s. Don't forget your invisible wands. Superhero capes are optional!

Focus Skill: counting by 10s to 100

Great for: moving while you learn

Materials

10 sheets of cardstock

Pencil

Scissors

Dot markers

Hole punch

Yarn

Directions to Make

1. Draw and cut out one hero shield from each sheet of cardstock.
2. Stamp 10 dots on each shield with the dot markers.
3. Hole punch one circle on the top of each shield.
4. Thread a 10-inch (25-cm) piece of yarn through the hole and tie in a loop to hang.

Directions to Play

1. Hang the hero shields across the backyard.
2. Select one hero shield to start. Tap your invisible hero wand at it and say 10.
3. Fly to the next hero shield. Tap it and say 20.
4. Keep flying, tapping and counting by 10s until each player reaches 100.

★ See photo on page 82 (upper left).

Game Variations

★ Place the hero shields on the ground in a circle. Walk and count.
★ Write the numbers in the shields instead of dots: 10, 20, 30, 40, 50, 60, 70, 80, 90, 100.
★ Focus on counting by 5s by putting 5 dots on each shield and making a total of 20 shields.

BEES IN THE HIVE

Shiny gem bees come to life as they buzz into their number hives with this hands-on math game to help children learn to recognize and group numbers. Players even have the chance to create beehives using recycled materials.

Focus Skill: counting groups of numbers 0 to 10

Materials

10 recycled plastic containers like milk cartons, juice containers or water bottles

ADULTS ONLY: Sharp knife to make opening in containers

Yellow and brown paint

Paint brush

Bubble wrap

Permanent black marker and yellow marker

Glass gems

Paper and marker (optional)

Directions to Make

1. Make beehives with recycled containers by having an adult cut out a hole in each container.
2. Paint the recycled containers yellow.
3. Create a beehive look by using bubble wrap dipped in brown paint and then stamping onto the recycled containers.
4. Create bees by using yellow and black markers on glass gems to make stripes and eyes.
5. Write a number on each hive from 0 to 10 or write on pieces of paper.

Directions to Play

1. Players take the bees and place the correct number into each beehive.
2. Players win when all the hives are filled with the correct number of bees.

Game Variations

★ Make beehives into word family hives and create word bees.

★ Create math fact bees to place into the correct beehives.

★ Add magnets to bees to create bees that can fly into their hives on a magnetic surface.

PATTERN SNAKE IN A SACK

Patterns can be found all around us. This backyard scavenger hunt for rocks can be a fun way to start exploring patterns and build critical-thinking skills. Players use painted rocks to create their own snake patterns.

Focus Skill: creating and extending patterns

Materials

27 smooth rocks of similar sizes

3 bigger-sized rocks for snake heads

3 colors of paint

Paint brushes

6 googly eyes

3 felt strips

Craft glue

Paper lunch sack or fabric bag

Directions to Make

1. Gather 27 rocks of similar sizes and three bigger-sized rocks.

2. Paint the three larger rocks to represent snake heads.

3. Attach googly eyes and a felt tongue to snake head with craft glue and allow to dry.

4. Using the three selected colors, paint the remaining rocks in sets of nine and allow to dry. When complete there will be nine of each color.

5. While the paint is drying, encourage your child to decorate the outside of the sack with the words "Snake in a Sack."

6. When the rock paint is dry, place the rocks in the bag.

Directions to Play

1. Each player selects a large snake head and places it on the floor in front of them.

2. Each player takes a turn selecting a rock from the bag to create a pattern snake.

3. They can choose to keep the color if it will help them create and extend a pattern.

4. If the color drawn from the bag doesn't match their pattern, they put it back and the next player draws.

5. The game ends when the first player is able to make a pattern snake with nine rocks.

Note

Rocks can be reused from the Rock Number Hunt activity on page 100 for this activity.

Game Variations

★ Make a vertical pattern using rocks to create pattern towers.

★ Younger players can use rocks to focus on number groupings.

★ Use rocks to outline a designated shape.

MOVE iT!

Get your wiggles out with this high-action counting game. Children draw an action card from one pile and a movement card from another, then perform that action. Use this math game in between sit-down lessons to give young children a chance to move and learn. When their bodies *do* math, they can develop a deeper connection to numbers. It is also a great game to informally assess children's understanding of numbers. If they draw the number 6 card, say 6 and jump 6 times, then you know that they understand what the number 6 is and how many it represents.

Focus Skill: recognizing and representing the numbers 0 to 20

Great For: moving while you learn

Materials

30 (3" x 5" [7.6 x 12.7-cm]) notecards

Pencil

Game Variations

★ Use the numbers 0 to 5 for beginning learners.

★ Have players draw two number cards and perform the action for the difference.

★ When playing in a large group, have two children draw the cards and the entire group perform the action.

Directions to Make

1. Write 10 movement actions on 10 of the notecards.

    a. Hop on one foot

    b. Run in place

    c. Skip

    d. Bend your knees

    e. Jump

    f. Reach up high

    g. Gallop

    h. Clap

    i. Twirl

    j. Touch the ground

2. Write the number 0 to 20 on the remaining notecards.

Directions to Play

1. Place the cards upside down in two separate piles.

2. Player one turns a number card over and says the number out loud.

3. Player two turns an action card over and reads the action out loud.

4. Both players stand up and do the action for the selected number of times.

5. Play continues for five or more rounds.

MAKE 10

Card games are a great way to bring more math into your everyday world in a fun way. Children can sort them by colors or numbers. You can put the cards in numerical order. You can even practice addition with cards. This activity has you adding the cards in many different ways to make 10. When you do find a way to make 10, discard your cards and flip more cards over from your pile. Be the first to turn over your pile of cards.

Focus Skill: making 10 when added to the given number

Materials

Deck of cards

Directions to Make

1. Remove the jacks, queens, kings and jokers from the deck of cards.

Directions to Play

1. Deal the cards facedown evenly to all players.

2. Each player turns over four cards and sets them to the right of their pile.

3. The youngest player goes first. They look over their cards for a way to make 10. Aces are equal to 1. If they can make the sum of 10, they pick the cards up and place them in a discard pile, then turn the cards from their pile over to fill in the spaces. If they cannot make 10, they choose one card to place at the bottom of the pile and turn one card over from their pile to fill the space. There will always be only four cards faceup in front of each child at all times.

4. The next player takes their turn, repeating step 3.

5. Play continues until one player has turned over all of his or her card pile.

Game Variations

★ Keep the cards totaling 10 separate. Write down the different ways to make 10 after each game.

★ Select a different number for players to make, such as 6. Allow them to use addition or subtraction to make the selected number.

★ Try the game with three or five cards turned faceup. Discuss the effect on the game. Does it make it easier or harder to make 10?

FILLING FISHBOWLS

There's a sale at the pet store for 10 goldfish and a bowl. Players count out 10 fish to fill each bowl for their customers, to practice counting in groups of 10. Using water beads, players practice counting from 0 to 10. Plus, as they count they set up groups to start developing skills of skip counting.

Focus Skill: grouping items into groups of 10 and skip counting

Materials

100-plus water beads

Large container filled with water

Paper

Markers

Scissors

10 clear small cups

Plastic scooper

Directions to Make

1. Soak the water beads in water to enlarge.
2. Use the paper and markers to make a pet store sign in the shape of a fish (i.e., $1.00 for 10 Fish)

Directions to Play

1. Players work to fill each cup "fishbowl" with 10 waterbead "fish" by scooping out of the large container filled with water beads.
2. Once all 10 cups are filled, encourage players to count by 10s to 100 to complete the sale.

Game Variations

★ Fill cups based on assigned numbers from 0 to 10.

★ Create number sentences to solve. Players respond with answer using water bead fish.

★ Create a sorting game for younger children by sorting water beads by color.

FLY BALL

Ding-dong! It's a special delivery. Luckily your box comes complete with packing paper! Don't just toss it in the recycle bin, rip the paper up into pieces and try your hand at Paperball. Let your kids toss the balled up paper high in the air and listen to their squeals of delight when their paper balls land in the box. This math game provides children with the opportunity to practice counting and answering the question, "How many?"

Focus Skill: counting and writing, "How many?"

Great For: moving while you learn

Materials

Paper (newspaper, tissue paper or packing paper)

Small box

Tape

String

Pencil

1 piece of lined paper

Directions to Make

1. Rip the paper into 10 larger pieces. Make paper balls with each piece.
2. Set a box out.
3. Measure 8 feet (2.4 M) from the box and tape or set a string at that distance for the throwing line.

Directions to Play

1. Stand facing the box with your toes behind the line.
2. Throw each paper ball toward the box.
3. How many balls landed in the box? Count the number of balls that land inside.
4. Write the number of balls that land in the box on the recording sheet.
5. Repeat steps 1 to 4 for another five rounds. As the game continues, mix things up by varying the distance from the box. Throw from various positions, such as standing, sitting or even lying down!

Game Variations

★ Write a number on each ball. Throw them into the box in numerical order.

★ Turn the box on its side and try to kick the paper balls in.

★ Use only four paper balls and call out the fraction of balls that landed in the box.

TAP AND TOSS

Watch out, this math game creates giggles galore, while providing your little ones with an opportunity to skip count by 2s to 100. Let your balloon fly to the sky as the children count on by 2s until the balloon drops.

Focus Skill: counting by 2s to 100

Great for: moving while you learn

Materials

Inflated balloon

Directions to Play

1. Toss the balloon in the air to start the game. Tap the balloon back in the air one time and whisper the odd number. 1—tap. On the second tap, say the number out loud and toss it in the air toward a team member. 2—toss.

2. They tap the balloon in the air, whispering the number. 3—tap. Then they toss it high in the air toward another team member and say the even number out loud. 4—toss.

3. Try to make it to 100. If the balloon drops, start over at the nearest multiple of 10.

Game Variations

★ Challenge the players to play the game without saying the odd numbers.

★ Have children play on their own.

★ For younger learners, have them toss the balloon and say the numbers in sequential order.

★ Practice counting by 5s. Tap four times quietly and toss on the fifth.

LUCK OF THE DRAW

In this game, your child will pick a number card from the pile and read it. Then, they will have to do that number of items for their chores. Admittedly, one may argue this may not be the "funnest" game for your child, but it's sure fun for the adults! This game works well when folding clothes and tidying up toys. As much "fun" as it is, it really is a great way to teach counting by ones to a higher number.

Focus Skill: counting objects by matching each number with a specific object

Great For: moving while you learn

Materials

Deck of cards with the face cards removed

Directions to Play

1. Select a specific chore.
2. Hold the cards facedown.
3. Let the child select a card.
4. Read the number out loud. Pick up and count that specific amount of objects.
5. The next player repeats steps 2 to 4 until the chore has been completed.

Game Variations

★ If you have a lot of objects that need picking up, consider having the child draw two cards and pick up the same number of objects as the sum.

★ Have them select two cards and pick up the difference.

★ Add in the face cards and assign them a special task. Draw a jack and you get to sweep the floor! The queen means you must pick up 10 items left-handed, the king right-handed.

SHAPE MEMORY

The great thing about this game is that you do not need any fancy supplies or game cards; just grab a pack of play dough from your craft supply closet and play! My kids usually last about five rounds of the game, or 20 minutes. It is a great game for siblings to play at the dinner table while you are preparing dinner.

Focus Skill: building and identifying three-dimensional shapes

Materials

Play dough

Paper cups

Directions to Make

1. Build two sets of three-dimensional shapes out of play dough: cube, pyramid, sphere, cone, cylinder. There will be 10 total shapes made.

Directions to Play

1. Count out 10 cups.

2. Hide one three-dimensional shape under each cup.

3. Mix the cups.

4. The youngest player starts first and turns over two cups. If the shapes match, they keep the pair. If they do not, they say the name of the shape out loud and turn the cups over.

5. The play continues to the right until all pairs have been found.

Game Variations

★ Start with only six cups and three pairs of shapes.

★ Turn the cups right side up and play the game with the shapes visible.

★ For an additional challenge, make two-dimensional shapes as well and increase the amount of shape pairs used.

SHAPE TILES

Is it a rocket, a cat or a tree? Players use magnetic shape tiles to create their own new shapes with this hands-on magnetic game. This playful game teaches a child to create objects from a variety of shapes.

Focus Skill: creating a shape out of smaller shapes

Materials

24 square pieces of cardstock

Markers or paint and paint brush

Magnetic tape

Magnetic surface

Directions to Make

1. Draw portions of shapes on the paper tiles with the markers or paint. Make six half circles, six right triangles, six squares and six rectangles.
2. Attach magnetic tape to the back of each paper tile.

Directions to Play

1. Each player takes a turn creating a shape out of the magnetic paper tiles to form a bigger shape on a fridge or other magnetic surface.
2. Challenge players to create another shape using two, three or even four tiles together.
3. The player who can create the most shapes wins.

Game Variations

★ Have each player create a pattern using the shape tiles.

★ Create a "tell a story" game using the tiles and have children describe the story.

★ Copycat shapes. Each player re-creates the image created on paper using magnetic shapes.

MYSTERY MATH

This math game requires no preparations and is great for groups of three of more children. Try this while waiting in line for an event or sneak in one round in-between lessons.

Focus Skill: solving addition equations

Materials

None

Directions to Play

1. Two children stand back to back and hold up any number of fingers.

2. A third child, the Math Master, looks at both numbers and calls out the sum.

3. The children then race to figure out which number the other is holding up. The first player to guess the correct number wins. The winner becomes the Math Master.

4. The children return to the group and two different children stand back to back and repeat steps 1 to 3.

Game Variations

★ Play with the numbers 0 to 5 by limiting the game to the use of just one hand.

★ Have a fourth player write the number sentence on a large chart after the answer has been called.

★ As an extra challenge, the Math Master can call out the difference of the numbers.

CUPCAKE SHAPES

Decorating cupcakes can be such fun! Add some shapes to create a playful learning game that can extend to various skills needed to prepare for school. Players create cupcakes by attaching matching shape pieces onto hanging contact paper to help learn their shapes.

Focus Skill: recognizing shapes

Materials

Construction paper

Scissors

Contact paper

Tape

Sequins, glitter or confetti

Directions to Make

1. Create six large cupcake shapes using a half circle of colored construction paper for the top to represent cupcake frosting.

2. Cut out six pyramid shapes for the cupcake liner. Fold paper accordion style to give it the cupcake-liner look if you'd like.

3. Cut out and place a shape in the middle of each liner (circle, triangle, square, rectangle, diamond or star).

4. Cut out multiples of each shape for game pieces and cover them with contact paper.

5. Attach the cupcakes to a wall or window with tape.

6. Cover the cupcakes with contact paper with the sticky side up.

Directions to Play

1. Players select shapes from the pile and match to the correct shape by placing onto the cupcake frosting area.

2. Continue to match shapes to each cupcake until all the shapes are attached correctly.

3. Players can also add cupcake decorations with confetti, glitter or sequins.

4. Continue playing by removing and mixing up shapes and then re-sorting.

Game Variations

★ Create cupcakes for number recognition.

★ Create cupcakes for uppercase and lowercase recognition.

★ Create cupcakes based on letter sounds.

PARACHUTE SUBTRACTION

Set aside one day every week to bring out your parachute. There are so many fun gross motor and math games to play, and the kids LOVE parachute time. It is a much anticipated activity in our homes and classrooms. This math game focuses on learning and practicing simple subtraction. Throw in a few soft foam balls and start shaking!

Focus Skill: simple subtraction

Great For: moving while you learn

Materials

Parachute or circular vinyl table cloth

10 soft foam balls

Directions to Play

1. Spread the parachute out and space children out evenly around it.
2. Shake, move and play for five minutes prior to starting the game.
3. When ready, count and throw 10 balls into the middle of the parachute.
4. Shake the parachute to the count of 10, trying to keep the balls in the middle.
5. Stop.
6. Count the number of balls that fell off. Say the number sentence to represent what happened. If 3 balls fell off, you would say: $10 - 3 = \_\_$?
7. Have the children call out the answer.
8. Throw all 10 balls back into the middle of the parachute and repeat.

Game Variations

★ Add more or fewer balls to change the level of difficulty.

★ Shake foam letters instead of balls. See which letters remain on the parachute.

★ Use balloons and write the numbers on each with a permanent marker.

GROCERY STORE

Learning coin names and values can be empowering for young children. In this game, shoppers use their grocery cart and money to purchase items at the store. This activity allows players to pretend and get creative with math.

Focus Skill: identifying coins and their monetary value

Materials

Grocery store flyers, magazines or newspaper ads

Scissors

Black marker

3" x 5" (7.5 x 13-cm) notecards

Crayons or markers

Paper for store banner

4 lids per player

7 pipe cleaners per player

1 small box per player

Coins (penny, nickel, dime, quarter)

Directions to Make

1. Players cut out pieces from each food group from the flyers.

2. Write on each notecard a price for each food item and display in the pretend store.

3. Using crayons or markers, create a banner for the store and hang up.

4. Each player creates their own grocery cart by attaching lids with pipe cleaners for the wheels. Attach pipe cleaners onto the box to make the handle. Decorate your cart (box) with crayons or markers. (Kids will need adult help to create.)

Directions to Play

1. Each player takes a turn selecting an item from display and adds it to their cart.

2. Player gives the storekeeper player the money for the item from their money pile.

3. Players continue to take turns shopping until all the items and/or money are gone.

Game Variations

★ Have players add up the values of their items and then make a payment.

★ Have players write a list of items and then purchase them from the store to encourage writing.

★ Challenge players to find specific food groups on their turn.

MEMORY PHOTO SHAPES

Children love to see images of themselves. This memory shape game uses photos to give them a whole new way to learn about shapes. Players discover matches by using visual discrimination.

Focus Skill: identifing name of shapes

Materials

Photos

Construction paper

Scissors

Glue stick

Directions to Make

1. Take images of your child and print the photos.
2. Cut out outlines on 4-inch x 6-inch (10 x 15-cm) paper into the shapes of a circle, triangle, square, rectangle, diamond and star. Make two sets of each shape.
3. Overlay the shape outlines onto the child's photos and glue together.

Directions to Play

1. Lay out the photo shapes onto a flat surface with the image side down.
2. Players take turns selecting two photos at a time to find a shape match.
3. Players continue to draw pieces to match each shape.

Game Variations

★ Create patterns with the photo shapes.

★ Use a craft knife to cut out shapes from the photos and keep the 4-inch x 6-inch (10 x 15-cm) shape whole to use as the game piece. Use the removed shape as a puzzle piece for the child to solve the missing piece by shapes.

★ Create a number photo memory game.

2A

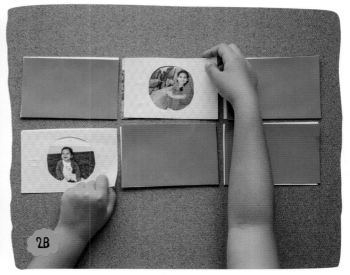

2B

FACT FAMILY CITY

Which street do you live on? Explore fact families in this playful skyscraper city game that helps children problem solve to discover which street the building is on by solving number sentences. Players are asked to sort buildings into groups based on the answers they solve on them while playing this game.

Focus Skill: identifying that various number combinations can equal the same number

Materials

Various colors of construction paper

Crayons

Scissors

Black marker

6 pieces of black paper, 2" x 11.5" (5 x 29 cm)

30 strips of yellow construction paper, ¼" x 1" (6 mm x 2.5 cm)

Glue stick

Directions to Make

1. Create several buildings with your child using the construction paper and crayons (approximately 2 inches x 4 inches [5 x 10 cm] in size).

2. Once complete, write number sentences equaling 6 or less on a section of the building, leaving a blank space for the answer (3 + 1, 5 – 1, 4 + 0, etc.).

3. Create five number streets using black paper strips by cutting them 2 inches x 11.5 inches (5 x 29 cm).

4. Write one number on each block from 1 to 6.

5. Cut out 30 small yellow strips and glue them to the black number streets. Use six strips on each street to indicate lane dividers.

Directions to Play

1. Place the number streets onto a flat surface in numerical order.

2. Place buildings assorted for players to choose from.

3. Players takes their turn by drawing a math fact building and placing it on the correct number street.

4. Each player takes a turn until all of the buildings have been used.

Game Variations

★ For younger children, create number buildings and place in numerical order.

★ Create buildings of different heights and line them on street by size.

★ For advanced players, increase the total sum of each street to make more challanging.

ROCK CLOCK MYSTERY

Telling analog time takes a lot of practice for young learners. This activity gets children building and interacting with the placement of numbers on a clock as well as moving the hands (sticks) around to set the time. Try your hand at building this rock clock and creating short time stories to solve.

Hint: You can paint the numbers on the back of the rocks from Pattern Snake in a Sack (page 107)!

Focus Skill: solving time story problems

Materials

12 rocks

Paint

2 sticks

Directions to Make

1. Paint the rocks.
2. Paint a number 1 to 12 on each rock. Allow to dry overnight. (The rocks from Rock Number Hunt on page 100 can also be used for this game.)

Directions to Play

1. Use the rocks to build a clock in the shape of a circle on a flat surface.
2. Set the sticks in the middle as the hour and minute hands.
3. One child tells a story with a time problem.

Sample

Sam went to the park at 8:00.

He stayed for 1 hour and then went home.

What time did he go home?

4. The player to the right uses the hands of the rock clock to show the answer.
5. If correct, then he gets to make up a time story. If incorrect, he must change the hands on the clock to show the correct time before telling the next story.

Game Variations

★ Set the hour and minute hands on the clock. Act out something you would typically do at that time of day.

★ Have one player call out a time and another player shows that time on the rock clock.

★ Mix the rocks and race to rebuild the rock clock.

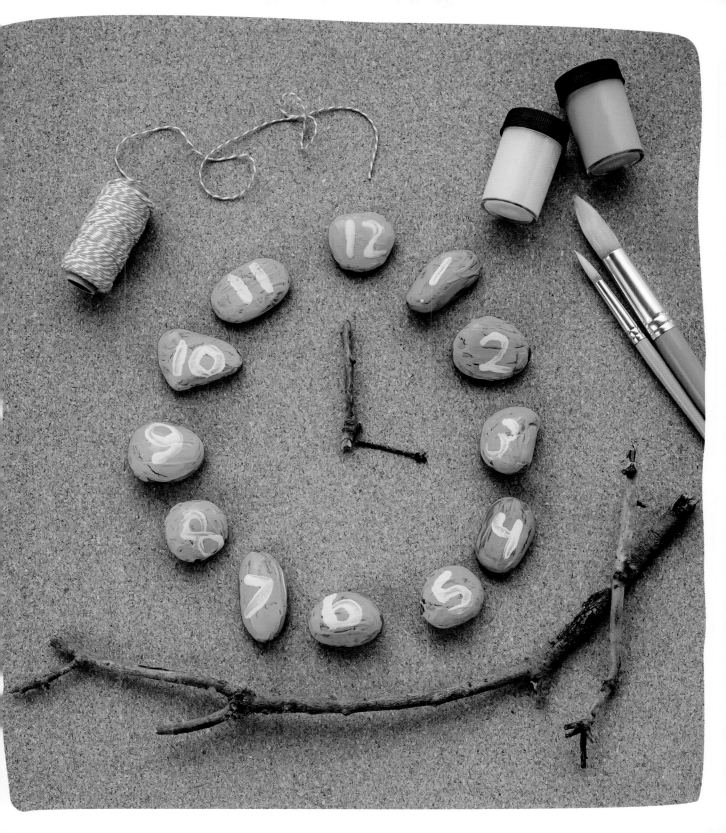

ESTIMATION STATION

Knowing how much space an object takes up is called special reasoning. This math skill is used when playing this estimation game along with an understanding of numbers. How close to the actual number can you guess? Set up this math learning center on a child-size table as an invitation to estimate.

Focus Skill: estimation

Materials

5 empty containers of varying sizes

Bricks or building blocks

Paper and pencil or number tiles

Directions to Make

1. Fill each container with bricks. Do not count.
2. Set the filled containers side-by-side on a table.
3. Place a paper and pencil or number tiles in front of each container.

Directions to Play

1. The first player stands in front of the first container. They make an educated guess, or estimate, of how many bricks they think are in the container. They write this number down on the paper or place their number tiles next to that container.
2. They move to the next container and repeat: estimate and write. The next player makes a number estimation at the first container. They write or place the number below the first player's guess.
3. The game continues until all players have written or placed their estimations for each container.
4. At the end, remove the bricks from each container. Count the number of bricks. The estimated number that is closest to the actual number of bricks wins. Draw a big star next to the winning number.

Game Variations

★ Play this game over a period of several days, allowing for one number entry per day.

★ Limit the number of containers.

★ Use a different filler, such as buttons, pom-poms or shape erasers.

SUPER SCIENCE

Young children are natural-born scientists. They observe and discover new things each day as they explore their surrounding environment. Making time for these moments is one of the best gifts you can give a child. Encourage them to share their observations and ask questions often about their discoveries. Science is all around us, from the insects in our backyard, plants in a garden, cooking in the kitchen, moon in the sky and even water play in the bathtub.

We can set up moments for observation by creating environments that foster opportunities for science. Provide science tools for discovery, like a magnifying glass, magnets and measuring cups, to help children learn to explore and test their science theories. A nature tray can be a fun place to start, with items you collect while taking a walk.

Here are a few games to play with your child to help them discover that science is all around them and to help build a solid foundation of science knowledge. The games are created to reinforce science standards that children are expected to learn as they enter school.

COMMUNITY CORNER

What is one reason why you feel doing science with your child is so important?

"I love doing science activities with my little ones because it not only provides a foundation for so many things they will encounter throughout their lives, but also sparks their curiosity to explore deeper and ask more questions."

—Dori W.

"Our children are much more likely to enjoy science and find it meaningful if we do hands-on science activities with them. I also believe in reading many science books that aren't textbooks. It's hard to develop a real love of science from a textbook."

—Deb C.

"Doing science together helps my children learn how to think, wonder and problem-solve. It encourages them to come up with their own questions and try to work out their own answers. I think they are really important skills that I want my girls to have to become successful adults."

—Cathy J.

"The kitchen is our laboratory. Cooking with children builds their knowledge and skills in science. Recipes can be science experiments that children can eat. Children learn about temperature, floating, sinking, dissolving, melting, freezing and measurements. They naturally learn what happens when you add liquid, temperatures reach a simmer or boiling, and so much more."

—Isabel R.

"Introducing the simple concept of asking questions, forming a hypothesis and testing within the parameters of a system like the scientific method is vital in elementary learning and is a foundation that must be intrinsic. When our daughter gets home from school, we rarely ask, 'What did you learn today?' Rather, it is more important for us to inquire, 'What questions did you ask today?'"

—Lin T.

"Starting science early on through observations, questions and hypothesizing, develops skills that will build a love of learning and discovery throughout their childhood and life. Whether it's growing beans in a jar or exploring rock pools on the shore the observing and trying to work out the why's, what's, when's and how's will lead to a lifelong love of science, exploration and discovery."

—Cerys P.

"It's important to teach science to our kiddos because it's the steppingstone of evolution and (what comes next) we want our kids to know everything they possibly can about the future."

—Tammi F.

"A lot of science for me is about noticing the world around us... then followed by thinking about it and understanding it a little. Turning our kids into thinkers and nurturing their natural curiosity. It is about exploration (together) and discovery. But it can also be a great humbling experience—we don't always need to know all the answers to life to enjoy it."

—Maggy W.

MAGNETIC CONSTRUCTION SITE

Create a moving construction site by placing select objects into this manipulative game. Players learn items can be magnetic and nonmagnetic as they discover the various selected items on the construction site. A basic skill of a scientist is how to classify and sort items.

Focus Skill: identifying that magnets can attract

Materials

Sand

Large plastic bin

Several magnetic items (bolts, nuts, metal containers, magnets, etc.)

Several nonmagnetic items (plastic figurines, Legos, coins, etc.)

Paper

Marker

Large magnet

Pretend construction vehicles

Directions to Make

1. Pour the sand into the large plastic bin for the base where objects will be hiding.

2. Place magnetic and nonmagnetic objects on the dirt (sand), hiding some within the sand if you like.

3. With the paper, create a game board with the words "magnetic" and "not magnetic" on it to sort items onto.

Directions to Play

1. Players take turns using the large magnet and construction vehicles to search for magnetic items.

2. As players remove items from the sand they will place them on the game board under the proper section of magnetic or not magnetic.

3. Continue to play until all of the items are classified.

Saftey Tip

Discuss safety rules about magnets with your child first. Store magnets out of reach. Monitor use at all times.

Game Variations

★ Race the clock to find all of the magnetic items at the construction site.

★ Dig for letters on the construction site and put in alphabetical order.

★ Dig for words on the construction site and sort into word families with like endings.

SENSES SCAVENGER HUNT

The rocks in the playground are bumpy. The leaves crinkle in the wind. Snacks of oranges smell sweet. In this science game, children use their keen observation skills to take note of the objects that demonstrate characteristics that can be noticed using the five senses.

✏️ **Focus Skill:** identifying and using the five senses

👟 **Great For:** moving while you learn

Materials

Paper

Pencil

Clipboard

Copier

Directions to Make

1. Write a list of object characteristics based on the five senses—touch, taste, smell, see and hear: bumpy, smooth, sweet, sour, red, green, purple, crinkles, dings.
2. Next to each characteristic, draw a small box.
3. Make a copy of this list for each player or small group of players.

Directions to Play

1. Walk around searching for items to match each characteristic.
2. When an item matching the description is found, check the box near the characteristic.
3. Continue playing the game until an object for each list item has been found.

Game Variations

★ Gather the items ahead of time and place them in a basket.

★ Have children write the object next to the describing word.

★ Focus on just one sense and the vocabulary words to describe those items.

GROWING A VEGETABLE GARDEN

Use colorful play dough to grow vegetables in your own pretend garden. Do you know where to find the vegetables that are ready to be picked? Players create vegetables and the plants they come from on the mat to re-create where and how they grow. This game helps a child learn to discover that vegetables are not from a store but from the earth, grown in a particular way.

Focus Skill: identifying major parts of plants (e.g., roots, stem, leaf, flower)

Materials

Marker

1 large piece of paper

Plastic cover sheet or laminate paper

12 squares of paper, 1.5" x 1.5"
(3.8 x 3.8 cm)

Play dough in vegetable colors

Directions to Make

1. Discuss the parts of a plant and how they grow with your child.
2. Draw a line on the paper to indicate the ground for the play dough garden to grow. Place paper inside of cover sheet.
3. Write the numbers 0 to 11 on the square cards.

Directions to Play

1. Say a type of vegetable out loud. Pick a number card.
2. Make that many vegetables of that kind in your garden. Be sure to include the roots, stem, leaf and flower, if applicable.
3. Repeat until you have a vegetable garden filled with play dough vegetables.

Game Variations

★ Create the vegetables in numerical order.
★ Make groups of different vegetables. Compare using "like" or "as."
★ Change the theme to fruit and create number trees.

ROCKET SHIP ADVENTURE

Launch your rocket ship into space to discover the sun, moon, stars and even the planets as you race to make it back to Earth in time. Players learn to identify and recognize items that are found in space.

Focus Skill: identifying elements of night, day and space

Great For: moving while you learn

Materials

Recycled cardboard box and recycled items

Markers

Paper

Scissors

3" x 5" (7.6 x 12.7-cm) index cards

Tape

Sand timer

Directions to Make

1. Players build and decorate a rocket ship out of a recycled cardboard box.
2. Create or print images of elements in space including the sun, stars, planets and phases of the moon. Feel free to add a few images of rockets, astronauts, comets, etc. to add more space fun.
3. Create smaller images and write the words to make game cards on the index cards and place into a pile.
4. Arrange or hang up the images from space around the room with tape.

Directions to Play

1. Player selects an index card from the pile and tells the other player to race the rocket to collect that space element and bring it back to mission control on Earth. Set the timer for each time the player leaves Earth.
2. Each player continues to take turns selecting objects from space from the cards and racing to bring them back to Earth.
3. The game continues until all the elements of space have been selected and returned to Earth.

Game Variations

★ Using many players, have two rockets that race to each space element by having one player sit inside the rocket and the other player push it.

★ Collect from your rocket images of the moon phases in order.

★ Collect from your rocket images of the planets in order from the sun.

ANIMAL SOUNDS BOWLING

Each animal has a unique name for children to discover and learn about. Use baby animal names and sounds to identify the grown-up animal in a unique twist on the game of bowling. Moo and meow along as you explore the science of animals.

Focus Skill: classifying and identifying animals and their young

Great for: moving while you learn

Materials

Paper

Markers

10 recycled plastic water bottles

Tape

Ball

Directions to Make

1. Draw or print out images of baby animals and adult animals (cow, calf, pig, piglet, duck, duckling, etc.).
2. Write the name of the animal under each picture.
3. Attach adult animal images onto front of bottles with tape.
4. Place baby animals in a pile to draw from.

Directions to Play

1. Players set up the adult animal bottles at the end of the area.
2. One player draws a baby animal image and calls out the animal sound.
3. The other player uses the ball to try to knock down the bottle with the adult animal on it.
4. Players take turns trying to knock down the animals based on animal sounds.

Game Variations

★ Write the word on the card to select and then attach image onto the bottles.

★ Attach animal pictures onto balls and as player picks up the ball they find the matching bottle to try to knock down.

★ Players select card from animal images and then they try to find the word written with chalk on sidewalk.

MAKE IT SINK

Children are intrigued by water and how items interact with it. Encourage science exploration by seeing who can make their container sink the fastest. A skill we ask young scientists to focus on is to compare and contrast their observations, and water creates the perfect environment to do that.

Focus Skill: identifying objects that sink or float

Materials

Large plastic container

Water

Large tray

Bolts

Nuts

Coins

Plastic beads

Pom-poms

Sand

Rocks

Any other small objects that can get wet

Small plastic containers with lids or plastic eggs

Directions to Make

1. Fill the large container with water.
2. Set objects on the large tray for players to select from.

Directions to Play

1. Players take turns using the items from the tray to fill their plastic container.
2. Players attach the lids and place into the water. Each player tries to see how quickly they can get their container to sink.

Game Variations

★ Players select a specific number of items to fill their container with to see who can make it sink first.

★ Players select the most amount of items to make their container float.

★ Players select the least amount of items to make their container sink.

Fizzing Fact Families

Add a little fizz to numbers to play this learning game focused on creating fact families with your child. Bonus is for players to discover that properties can change when you mix two ingredients.

Focus Skill: observing the changes in the properties of matter

Materials

3″ x 5″ (7.6 x 12.7-cm) index cards

Black marker

2 small squirt bottles

Baking soda

Kool-Aid packet

Water

Large rectangular container

Directions to Make

1. Write math facts on the index cards, leaving the answer off. For example, write 1 + 1 = ___.
2. Fill one squirt bottle with baking soda and the other with Kool-Aid powder and water.
3. Set up a large container to squirt contents into.

Directions to Play

1. The player selects a math fact card from the pile.
2. To solve the equation the player writes the answer with the squirt bottle filled with baking soda into the large container.
3. If the answer is correct the player uses the liquid squirt bottle filled with Kool-Aid to make a special scientific reaction. The reaction of the two ingredients combined produces a gas called carbon dioxide (CO_2), which creates bubbles. This process is called carbonation.
4. Players continue to solve math equations and form fizzing number solutions until all of the cards have been solved.

Note

Consider playing this bubbling science game in an area that's safe for potential colorful spills.

Game Variations

★ Younger players can find number matches and then create a fizzing number.

★ Players can find number matches and then make number dots to match the number for counting.

★ Advanced players can create multiplication number sentences and create a number fizz with the answer.

2 + 4 =
1 + 2 =
1 + 1 =

2

1 + 1 =

2 + 1 =

1 + 2 =

3

ICE CASTLE CHALLENGE

Who can create the tallest ice castle? Using strategic thinking, players can create their own ice structure that will last the test of gravity and heat.

Focus Skill: understanding that properties change with heat

Materials

Water

2 to 4 ice trays

Various small-size containers

Food coloring (optional)

2 large trays or cookie sheets

Paper

Pencil

Directions to Make

1. Pour water into ice cube trays and various shaped containers (food coloring optional).

2. Place in freezer overnight.

Directions to Play

1. Challenge players to build the tallest ice castle onto large trays or cookie sheets with the provided ice blocks and water.

2. Encourage players to design structures that will withstand the challenge of heat in a sunny location.

3. Create castle and set timer and observe the changes that occur over time.

4. Keep a record of how long each ice castle stands to determine the winner.

Note

Food coloring may stain.

Game Variations

★ Create a castle as a group building together.

★ Create an ice castle with additional materials such as bricks, gems, counters, etc.

★ Drip warm water on top to challenge the design and see how long it can stand.

LIFE CYCLE BLOCKS

Children are fascinated by nature's life cycles. Race the clock to see who is the fastest at creating a life cycle tower. The game helps a child learn to recognize and verbalize the patterns all around us in nature.

 **Focus Skill:** identifying patterns in life cycles

Great For: moving while you learn

Materials

5 to 10 sheets of white paper

Crayons or markers

Scissors

4 recycled square tissue boxes or recycled cardboard to make boxes

Tape

Sand timer

Directions to Make

1. Draw images or print from a computer the life cycles of frogs, butterflies, chickens, flowers, people or apple trees onto paper the size of your box.

2. Cut the life cycle stages apart from paper.

3. Gather the tissue boxes or see page 72 for how to make boxes with recycled cardboard.

4. Attach each image onto the sides of the boxes with tape so that both boxes match. Each box only gets one portion of the life cycle.

Directions to Play

1. Each player takes turns racing the sand timer to stack up the selected life cycle in order. For example, a completed life cycle for the butterfly would have an egg, caterpillar, chrysalis and butterfly with all four boxes stacked on top of each other in order.

2. Encourage players to name the stages of their chosen life cycle once their stack is complete.

3. Knock over and repeat.

Game Variations

★ Use varied-size boxes to match sizes during life cycles to create a tiered tower.

★ Stack up similar stages in the life cycles.

★ Sort images on the rug and place in chronological order.

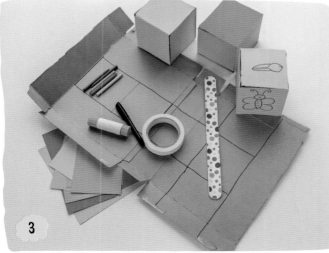

MONSTER FOOD GROUPS

Use your grocery store flyers and magazines to help your child learn about food groups with these adorable food group monsters. Players quickly learn which food groups fuel their body with energy and help them grow.

✎ **Focus Skill:** learning to identify food groups

Materials

Construction paper

Paper bag

Glue

Googly eyes

Scissors

Grocery flyers or magazines

Directions to Make

1. Use construction paper to create five monsters on paper bags. Attach paper with glue.
2. Add googly eyes to increase the monster effect.
3. Cut out an opening in the bag for a mouth to feed.
4. Label each bag with a food group: fruits, vegetables, dairy, grains and proteins.
5. Encourage players to cut out pictures of food groups from the flyers.

Directions to Play

1. During each player's turn they select a food item and feed the correct food group monster.
2. Players continue until all the food has been fed to the food group monsters.

Game Variations

★ Create a book about what your monster can eat featuring healthy options from the monster food groups.

★ For advanced players, add a point value to food groups to help build a foundation in nutrition.

★ Sort images of foods by feeding number monsters.

WATER BEAD RACE

Race your water beads to see which surface is the fastest using ramps and force to challenge your competitor. Begin to explore basic science concepts by using forces and inclined planes as a type of simple machine.

Focus Skill: understanding that the movement of objects requires force

Materials

Water beads

Water

Plastic container

Pool noodles or variety of flat materials for ramps

ADULTS ONLY: knife

Directions to Make

1. Soak water beads in water in a container to expand.
2. Have an adult cut pool noodles in half in various sizes.

Directions to Play

1. Players close their eyes to select materials to create a water bead ramp.
2. Using the selected item, each player designs their own ramp.
3. Players race each round to see whose design has the fastest incline by placing water bead onto the design ramp.
4. Provide additional challenge rounds by removing ramps and using air as the force.

Game Variations

★ Challenge players to see who can make their water bead travel the farthest.

★ Challenge players to have their water bead stop on a chosen target.

★ Add additional difficulty by increasing the number of ramps required to build for a race.

SUPERHERO WATER

Can you measure superpowers? In this activity, kids create their own superheroes by carefully measuring water into their superhero cups. They practice using standard measurement units as they build a superhero from the bottom up, adding a new feature at every ¼-cup (60-ml) mark. See how fast you can build your superhero!

Focus Skill: identifying and using standard units of measurement

Materials

Foam

Scissors

2 clear cups for each player

Black permanent market

Bucket

Water

Directions to Make

1. Prepare a water-friendly area for the game.

2. Using the foam, cut out a set of superhero capes, masks, belts and belt buckles for each player. Vary the superhero designs if desired.

3. For each player, take one clear cup and use the black permanent market to make small lines indicating ¼ cup (60 ml), ½ cup (118 ml), ¾ cup (177 ml) and 1 cup (237 ml). This will be the player's superhero cup.

4. Set another clear cup next to the superhero cup for each player. This cup will be used to pour the water.

5. Fill the bucket with water and place it where all the kids can access it easily.

Directions to Play

1. Players will dip their clear cup into the bucket of water then carefully pour "superpower water" into their superhero cup. When they reach a specific marking, they have to stop and add a superhero accessory. ¼ cup (60 ml) = belt, ½ cup (118 ml) = buckle, ¾ cup (177 ml) = cape, 1 cup (237 ml) = mask. The foam will stick to the measuring cup when you add water to the surface.

2. Players continue to pour the superpower water and build their superheroes. Race to see who is the fastest to make a complete superhero!

Game Variations

★ Create nonstandard units of measurement by using water bottles instead and pour to specific lined levels to create a superhero.

★ See which superhero bottle can fly the farthest when filled up with various levels of water.

★ Add different colors to the water to mix to create color superheroes.

MAGICAL MUSIC & ART

Exploring the arts with your child can be magical. A trip to an art museum or to a musical performance can be the highlight of their week. Look in your community for opportunities to be engaged in the arts. As you explore, help your child discover the patterns in a piece of art or the music you're listening to. Ask them how an art piece makes them feel. Challenge them to re-create what they see and hear when they return back home. Help increase their language and observation skills by encouraging a child to describe the details of their work. Celebrate their efforts as you become a child's No. 1 fan. Most importantly, give children the opportunity and tools to be expressive and creative!

We are sharing with you games that are meant to expose children to music and art. Throughout this book you will find that we incorporate these topics into many learning games as well. Using a variety of your child's senses can help them to learn things more effectively. Plus, using art and music can add an element of fun and creativity to everyday moments!

COMMUNITY CORNER

What is your favorite musical instrument to play with your child?

"My favorite instrument to play with my kids is the (Peruvian/Indian) spin drum. It's a two-sided folk drum you roll in your hands. I had one when I was young and loved it; it stuck with me and now they love it too."

—Kimberly H.

"I LOVE rain sticks for kids of any age."

—MaryAnn K.

"Our favorite instruments are our voices! We sing all the time together."

—Melissa L.

"I had my kids taking music lessons at a young age (starting at four). My sister is a piano teacher and convinced me that kids can learn formally at a young age; just find the right teacher and keep the lessons short, to just 15 minutes. After a few years of piano without much success, my kids all switched instruments to what they chose themselves. Music after that became more enjoyable for them. My girls switched to flute and my son to acoustic guitar. I think the empowerment of choosing your instrument and deciding the level of commitment to practice made my life easier and my kids happier too."

—Mia W.

"We use shakers and wood sticks for our favorite. Shakers we do a lot of dancing with. Wood sticks we tap out rhymes and patterns."

—Cassie H.

"The floor drums where all three of my kids can play together. We sing songs and take turns dancing while others drum."

—Meredith D.

"The radio. We have dance parties in the living room when we are mad. It helps keep the focus away from ourselves and we dance it all out. I also sing ridiculous songs about food at the grocery or when cooking to keep the toddlers calm."

—Meghan C.

"My favorite instruments for young children are those in the percussion family. I LOVE the cause-and-effect immediacy of picking up shakers and creating sound. Children delight in their ownership of following the beat. Percussion instruments lend themselves to whole-body movement and dance in response to music. Can't have enough!"

—Debbie C.

SiNG AND SHAKE

Stomp to the beat as you float the parachute up high! This music and movement game is a great activity for children to work together as a team to respond to a variety of different motions. It provides children with an interactive way to respond to music through singing and motion.

Hint: Use this activity along with Parachute Subtraction (page 122)!

Focus Skill: responding to music through singing and motion

Great For: moving while you learn

Materials

Parachute

Directions to Play

1. Children stand evenly spaced around the parachute. One child picks a movement to add to the song, such as stomp your feet.

2. The group sings and performs the selected movement. The next child then has a turn to call out the movement.

3. The game continues until all children have had the opportunity to call out a movement to add into the song.

Game Variations

★ Switch a balloon for a parachute and sing, "When the balloon goes up high…"

★ Write the action words on paper to tie in reading.

★ Change the words of the song to focus on counting. "When the parachute shakes high, stomp 3 times."

To the tune of "If You're Happy and You Know It"

When the parachute shakes high, stomp your feet.

When the parachute shakes high, stomp your feet.

When the parachute is high, floating up into the sky,

When the parachute shakes high, stomp your feet.

Alternate Ideas

Tiptoe

Wiggle your hips

Shake your head

Yell "Hooray"

FOLLOW THE LEADER

Let your child lead this game by making music in their own special way: high, low, fast or slow. Experiment with a variety of tempos and patterns in music. Take a turn being the leader too and demonstrate new ways to play. Show them how to tap hard and soft to create different sounds. Tap on different places on the oatmeal container. Does it sound the same if you tap on the sides as if you tap the top?

Focus Skill: experimenting with ways to make music

Great for: moving while you learn

Materials

Scissors

Construction paper

Oatmeal container

Markers

Glue

Directions to Make

1. Cut the paper to fit around the oatmeal container.
2. Encourage your child to decorate the paper with markers.
3. Glue the paper to the outside of the oatmeal container.

Directions to Play

1. Select one player to go first. They will tap or play their oatmeal drum and the rest of the players will copy their movements.
2. After a minute, change leaders. Encourage children to vary how fast or slow they play their oatmeal drum.

Game Variations

★ For advanced learners, teach them about notes and rests. Encourage them to make patterns such as tap-tap-rest with their drum.

★ Stand up and march around the room while playing. Let the leader go first.

★ Experiment with a variety of instruments such as shakers, rain sticks and bells.

FAST AND SLOW ART

Use your listening and creative skills to create your own art based on exploring the music beat. Players discover just how slow and fast music can be in a visual way.

Focus Skill: identifying changes in a pattern of music from fast to slow

Materials

Paint

Paper plates or container

Paper

Paint brush

Sponge

Music player

Directions to Make

1. Place paint onto a plate and lay out one sheet of paper per player.

Directions to Play

1. Players listen to the music and are challenged to paint with slow brush strokes with slow music and fast taps when music is fast.

2. Use a sponge to print up and down with the beat of the music.

3. Allow the paper to dry and hang the game up to enjoy their artwork.

Game Variations

★ Using pre-painted pieces, encourage players to dance based on the painting style they are shown.

★ Create a music masterpiece by rolling out a long sheet of paper and allow players to paint with their feet as the music changes from fast to slow, altering their steps.

★ Play music and encourage players to make movements that match the speed of the music.

KEEP A STEADY BEAT

Bring out the oatmeal drum that your child created in Follow the Leader (page 160) for this music and movement game. The leader will tap out a steady beat and the children will respond by moving their feet to the music.

 Focus Skill: playing instruments and moving to demonstrate awareness of beat

Great For: moving while you learn

Materials

Oatmeal drum

Directions to Play

1. One child starts as the leader. They select a steady beat and consistently tap that beat. Tap, tap, tap, tap.

2. The other children respond to the beat by moving their feet and walking, hopping, running, jumping or tiptoeing around the room. Tap the drum slowly for a walk, fast for a run and tap on the rim for a tiptoe.

3. When the music stops, the children freeze.

4. Repeat with another child as the leader.

Game Variations

★ Play this game with a variety of musical instruments such as maracas and bells.

★ Play music on the radio and have children move to the beat.

★ Provide each child with an instrument. Have all the players move and shake to the same beat.

WHERE IN THE WORLD

Discover that instruments and rhythms from various parts of the world have different sounds. Players explore different regions and celebrate the diversity in music.

Focus Skill: identifying various styles of music from around the world

Materials

10 music samples featuring instrumental and vocal music from around the world

Black paper

Scissors

World map

Directions to Make

1. Using online resources, find music samples from around the world.
2. Cut out 10 music notes per player, using black paper.

Directions to Play

1. Before game begins, play music with the children and share with them what continent each style of music belongs to by placing a note on the specific continent.
2. Each player gets 10 music notes to place on the continent when they listen to the 10 selections of music.

Game Variations

★ Match images of people dancing around the world with the music when played.

★ Cut out outlines of the continents to place on region where various music styles are played.

★ For advanced players, provide countries for them to select when they hear the selected pieces of music.

OUTDOOR SOUND GARDEN

Children explore the way items sound when you use a variety of materials to bang together. Go outdoors and create a sound garden and challenge players to grow their own sound patterns.

Focus Skill: identifying patterns in sounds

Materials

Variety of recycled kitchen items (colander, muffin tin, ice cube tray, spatula, whisk, etc.)

Optional: wood wall to attach items to

Paper

Black marker

Directions to Make

1. Gather materials and arrange outdoors on soft grass or a blanket or attach to a wood wall.
2. Create sound pattern cards by drawing images of recycled kitchen items in various patterns (muffin tin, ice cube tray, muffin tin, ice cube tray, etc.).

Directions to Play

1. Allow players to experiment with the sounds of the variety of recycled kitchen items.
2. Have players create repetitive patterns using their kitchen utensils on the kitchen items.
3. The next player tries to replicate the sound pattern of first player.
4. Using sound pattern cards, each player takes turns copying the images on the cards to create sound patterns.

Game Variations

★ Players work to find the sound garden items with the lower sounds.
★ Players work to find the sound garden items with the higher sounds.
★ Players create their own sound patterns and write on paper for other players to duplicate.

PRINT MYSTERIES

Did you ever wonder how an artist did that? Children analyze pieces of art to discover what tools they used to create the impressions on the canvas. Players use their own artwork to create a memory game.

Focus Skill: identifying objects used to create art prints

Materials

Variety of random objects for printing (sponge, scrubber, toothbrush, potato masher, bolt, lids, marbles, pipe cleaner, cookie cutter, ball of paper, paper clip, cup, magnetic letter, etc.)

Tray

Paint

Paper

Pencil

Directions to Make

1. Each player selects one object from the tray to dip into paint and stamp on their paper to create a piece of art. Write on the back of the paper what object they used to make the print with. (The game works best with 15 to 20 pieces of completed art.)

Directions to Play

1. Play a guessing game with players by having them pick up a painting and find which object on the tray created the prints with paint. Return the object to the tray.

2. The game continues until a match has been made for all of the pieces of art.

Game Variations

★ Increase the difficulty of the game by covering the items used for players to guess from.

★ Add a few random items to the tray to try to trick the players.

★ Cut the paper in half once the painting is dry to create a matching game or cut in a few pieces to create a puzzle for players.

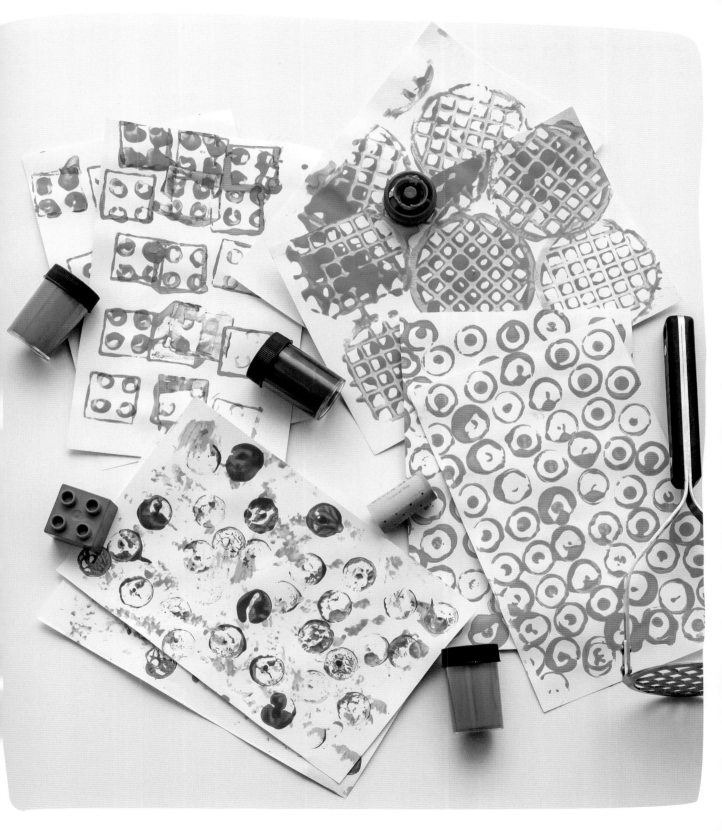

ROLL A SHAPE

Explore geometry through art with this playful art game. Not only will the children have a blast playing the game, they will also have a cute project to take home and hang on the refrigerator. It is a great game for playdates with large groups of children since it can be made ahead of time and is relatively low mess as far as art projects go!

Focus Skill: using geometric forms in a work of art

Materials

White multipurpose paper

Scissors

Square tissue box

Glue

Marker

Scrapbook paper

Large white paper

Directions to Make

1. Cut six white squares the same size as the tissue box. Glue one on each side. Draw a different shape on each side: square, rectangle, oval, circle, triangle, diamond.

2. Cut a variety of those shapes from scrapbook paper. Vary the sizes.

Directions to Play

1. One player shakes the die. The shape that is rolled may be selected from the pile of scrapbook paper shapes.

2. They pass the die to the next player and finish gluing the shape onto their large white paper.

3. Play continues for a minimum of six rounds.

Game Variations

★ Make the die with a focus on colors instead of shapes.

★ Use a variety of art mediums (crayons, stickers, markers, paint). Write the different choices on each side of the die.

★ Write a sentence that tells what to add to the picture such as: "Draw a zigzag."

ART DOMINOES

Children love to paint and create art. Create your own floor-sized art domino game with your child using their own marble paintings and focus on learning how to identify dot patterns.

 Focus Skill: using a variety of materials to create images

Great for: moving while you learn

Materials

Box or tray

Marble

Paint

Scissors

20 sheets of 8" x 11.5" (20 x 29-cm) cardstock

Glue

Directions to Make

1. Place a sheet of paper in the box or tray and then dip the marble into paint and roll around. Repeat with additional paint or various colors to create a design. Duplicate five times to have multiple pieces of painted paper and allow to dry.

2. Cut out 168 circles approximately 1 inch (2.5 cm) in diameter from the six painted sheets of paper to use for dots on the dominoes.

3. Cut 14 sheets of 8-inch x 11.5-inch (20 x 29-cm) paper in half to create art dominoes.

4. Glue circles onto cardstock in traditional domino pattern. Use dot patterns from 0 to 6. (Search online for sample layout if needed.)

Directions to Play

1. Place art dominoes in a pile and have each player select seven dominoes. Place the remainder of art dominoes in a pile to draw from. One player turns over the top card for beginning game piece.

2. Players hold art dominoes like cards and take turns laying down their cards to match the art domino piece on the floor. If unable to match a domino, player selects a new domino from the pile.

3. Play continues until a player has played all of their art dominoes.

Game Variations

★ Use recycled cereal boxes to create art dominoes that can stand up and make chain reactions just like the smaller version.

★ Join together two art dominoes to create number problems to solve.

★ Players race to place their selected pieces in numerical order based on total amount on art domino.

NIGHT AT THE MUSEUM

Experience your own night at the museum by discovering famous pieces of art with your special artist flashlight. This activity exposes children to art masterpieces at an early age to help to develop knowledge and appreciation.

Focus Skill: learning to identify different styles of art

Great For: moving while you learn

Materials

Printed images of famous pieces of art

Printed images of artist with image next to them

Flashlight

Directions to Make

1. Select and print 10 pieces of famous art from online images with your child.
2. Create a piece of paper for a scavenger hunt by placing an image of the famous artist and the piece of work beside them.
3. Add the text of the artist and artwork name to the scavenger hunt and discuss names with players.

Directions to Play

1. Hang the pieces of art around the room in a dim light setting.
2. Using the flashlight, encourage players to search around the room for the pieces of art in the museum.
3. Once a player finds a piece of art they check it off the list until they have found each piece of artwork.

Game Variations

★ Give each player an artist image and ask them to find the piece of art they created.
★ Create a memory game with the famous pieces of art selected.
★ Create a puzzle with each image for players to solve.

DRAGON CASTLE

Explore a time from long ago with a castle and one special dragon who likes to explore in all sorts of directions through the castle. Players learn to create a three-dimensional piece of art that becomes an inspiration for imaginary play. Plus adults can sneak in a little vocabulary as you encourage players to explore positional words.

Focus Skill: creating three-dimensional art

Materials

Cardboard box

Scissors

Markers

Paper

Egg carton

Googly eyes

Glue

Paint

Paint brush

3" x 5" (7.5 x 13-cm) index cards

Directions to Make

1. Remove the top pieces of the box and then cut out the edges to make the box look like the edges of a castle (adult task).

2. Add a doorway on top and two sides but keep the bottom so it can lift up and down for entrance.

3. Cut out windows on each side of the castle (or color with markers).

4. Decorate the castle with markers and paper to create stonework and plants surrounding castle.

5. Create a dragon using egg carton, googly eyes and paint.

6. Write on index cards directional words including beside, in front of, behind, on top of, above, between, inside and under.

Directions to Play

1. After players have created their three-dimensional piece of art, it's time to explore the castle.

2. Each player takes a turn by picking a positional word from the word pile and placing the dragon in the castle using the positional word chosen.

2. Players continue to take turns selecting positional word cards and placing dragon accordingly.

Game Variations

★ Play a hide-and-seek game by having one player hide a gold coin while the other one discovers it in the castle with the dragon and labels it with the correct positional word.

★ Hang famous pieces of art in the castle and have players draw cards with art and find the match.

★ Create a positional word book illustrating the dragon's position within the castle for a fun sight word book.

PATTERN WHEEL

There is something magical about a group of five to seven children all working together to complete a collaborative art project. I just love the hum of busy, happy kids expressing their creativity. This game is great for helping to develop a caring community of learners, creative expression and a little math too!

Try making a few wheels in varying sizes. Hang them from a clothesline or bulletin board for a festive display.

Focus Skill: using lines, shapes and forms to make patterns

Materials

Scissors

Large paper

Markers

Directions to Make

1. Cut a large circle from the paper.
2. Draw lines to divide the circle into six equal pieces.

Directions to Play

1. The first player closes their eyes and reaches into the marker container for a color.
2. The player to their right calls out a style of line or shape: zigzag, dots, squiggles, etc.
3. The first player then must use that style of line or shape in a pattern to decorate their part of the circle.
4. Play continues until all children have received one color marker and a style of line or shape to draw. They complete their section.
5. When the entire pattern wheel is complete, display!

Game Variations

★ Draw for two colors and let the player to the right call out two different styles of lines or shapes.

★ Switch a circle for another shape: pentagon, octagon or diamond.

★ Use stamps or paint instead of markers to explore a variety of art materials.

GOING GLOBAL

Young children start becoming globally aware by taking a closer look at the immediate world around them. They start to learn more about themselves, their family and their neighborhood. As this knowledge develops and grows, they are more able to grasp bigger concepts, such as what the world is and how to use a globe, and learn about other people's cultures and celebrations.

We make a point to allow our children to experience other cultures with food, art, crafts, music, geography, presentations and games. In addition to raising globally aware children, many families have also chosen to raise their children to be bilingual, introducing and using another language in their daily lives.

Here are just a few games to play with your children to get them thinking more globally. If your family does speak two (or more) languages, try playing these games in both languages.

 # COMMUNITY CORNER

What is your favorite learning material for teaching children about the world?

"A world map—no matter what we talk about, whether family, history, foods, animals, etc., we use our map to see where in the world it is found/is or how and where it has traveled."

—Cordelia N.

"We have just started to show our son some old postcards we have collected over the years. He is almost four years old and has been fascinated about both the people who sent them to us and where they have come from. He seems to prefer pictures with sky in them at the moment, but whatever they are he wants to know the country they came from and the language they speak there."

—Stephen G.

"A globe. We have quite a few globes around the house and we love looking at them. I also use one in particular on each occasion my husband goes on a business trip. He travels the world, so we have a look at where he is and has been, how far it is from home and where our families are in the world in relation to him."

—Annabelle H.

"Photographs. They love seeing our photographs of the places they have read about in books, learned about in school or heard about in movies. Seeing and holding the actual photo of the place or landmark, usually with their parents standing in the forefront, makes learning so much more fun and personal. It instills in them a desire to follow in our footsteps and discover the world too."

—Frances M.

"TV programs and the Internet. Having family literally on almost every continent of the world helps too!"

—Varya S.

"Always a map because we can link everything back to it—weather, coins, biomes/animals, cultures, food, etc. We look where they originate and talk about who they border, what their climate would be, if they have a coast, mountains, etc."

—Becky M.

"We make heavy use of our atlas. My son is five, and we refer to our atlas a lot in our home school studies, but also whenever we read or hear about another country."

—Leanna G.

WHERE IS THE DUCK?

Track your duck around the map using directional words to make it come back home. Children practice using the words *north, east, south* and *west* as their duck takes a journey through the oceans of the world.

Focus Skill: identifying north, south, east and west on a map

Materials

20 (1" x 3" [2.5 x 7.6-cm]) pieces of paper, plus more for creating ducks and home star

Scissors

Printed map of the Earth

Marker

Directions to Make

1. Create small ducks for each player with the paper. Create a paper star.
2. Print out or create a large map of the Earth.
3. Divide the map into 12 squares by folding.
4. Place the star on the map to use as the duck's home where you live.
5. Write the words *north, south, east* and *west* on 20 cards.

Directions to Play

1. Each player gets a duck and selects a side to start from.
2. Players draw a direction from the pile and move their duck in that direction one square over.
3. The players try to work their way to the star to end the game.

Game Variations

★ Challenge players to land on specific countries or continents to place their duck on.

★ Create multiple stopping points for the duck to collect on its journey around the world.

★ Have players choose from positional words around the map of the Earth.

TREASURE HUNT

Get kids excited about making and using a map with this fun treasure hunt game. This is a great activity for playdates and birthday parties. Stuff your treasure box with party goody bags for the kids to take home. Small erasers, spinning tops and stickers make great non-candy prizes.

Focus Skill: drawing and using a map; using relative location of people, places and things; using positional words

Great For: moving while you learn

Materials

2 empty boxes

Markers and stickers

Small treasure items

2 pieces of paper

Pencil

Directions to Make

1. Divide the children into two groups.

2. Let each group decorate a box with markers and stickers. Have them fill the box with the treasures when they are done.

3. Select an area for each group to make their map.

4. Let them choose a starting point based on the relative location to an object. Example: Start at the big oak tree. Draws a picture of a tree and writes the word start.

5. Have them draw a picture and/or write sentences to describe the steps taken to reach the treasure. Use prepositional words such as over, under, next to, above.

6. The directions should end at a place where the box can hide. Hide the box there.

Directions to Play

1. Select one team to go first. Give them the child-made map to follow.

2. Let them read and follow the directions to find the treasure. Cheer them on.

3. Once they have found the treasure, let the other team repeat steps 1 and 2.

Game Variations

★ Use word clues or picture clues only.

★ For younger learners, the adults may make the map and hide the treasure ahead of time.

★ For advanced learners, use a tape measure. Have them record the exact measurements between places.

LAND VS. WATER

Explore the differences between land and water on a globe with this game. Many party stores and some online stores will carry inflatable globes. If you can't find one, you can always make your own with a permanent marker and plain ball.

Focus Skill: distinguishing between land and water on maps and globes

Materials

Paper

Pencil

Inflatable globe

Directions to Make

1. Write a large "T" on the paper.
2. Add the words *water* and *land* to each side to make the game board.

Directions to Play

1. Assign one player to be the record keeper.
2. Toss the ball to another player. The child will catch the ball with two hands.
3. They will look to see where their right pointer finger lands and call out: "land" or "water."
4. The recorder will make a tally mark on that side of the paper.
5. Repeat steps 2 to 4 for a total of 20 tosses.
6. Add up each side tallies. Who won—land or water?

Game Variations

★ Write the specific name of the land or ocean each player points to.

★ For more advanced players, discuss how the earth is made up of more than 75 percent water and other world facts.

★ Play this game using a map. Close your eyes and point.

What kind things for others do you do on holidays?

CELEBRATION JAR

Children delight in talking about themselves and their families. This game gives them the chance to share more about their own celebrations while learning about others.

Focus Skill: recognizing and comparing celebrations and holidays of others

Materials

Scrapbook paper

Scissors

Pencil

Mason jar

Directions to Make

1. Cut colorful strips of paper.

2. Write a celebration question on each strip of paper. Sample questions include: What is your favorite holiday? How does your family celebrate birthdays? What winter holidays does your family celebrate? What is your favorite food to eat for Thanksgiving? What kind of gifts do you give to others on their birthday? What kind of gifts do you give others for holidays? How does your family decorate for the holidays?

3. Fold and place in the jar.

Directions to Play

1. The youngest player selects a question from the jar. With the help of an adult, they read the question and answer it.

2. Each player in the game then has a chance to answer it as well.

3. When everyone has answered the question, the next player draws a strip from the celebration jar and repeats steps 1 and 2.

Game Variations

★ For a speed game of celebrations, allow one-word answers.

★ Switch celebration questions for other themes: science topics, state facts, inspirational quotes or religious sayings.

★ Create a homemade board game with the questions instead of placing them in the jar.

STATE TOSS

Encourage children to explore the United States by tossing a rock onto various state outlines. Using a secret trick that artists use, create your own outline of the United States with chalk and focus on learning all 50 states.

 Focus Skill: identifying the states in the United States of America

Great For: moving while you learn

Materials

Map of the United States

Chalk

Rock

Paint

Paintbrush

Paper

Pencils

Directions to Make

1. Print out a map of the United States and fold into 16 squares.

2. Have an adult create a grid of 16 squares with chalk on the ground or place dots at the intersections.

3. Adults and players work together to re-create the map with chalk. Draw the lines represented in each grid on the printed paper onto the ground in the corresponding grid box or dot intersections depending on the method you select.

4. Paint a self-portrait with paint on the rock for game pieces.

5. Create a traveling tracking sheet for each player with text and image outlines of the states.

Directions to Play

1. Players take turns tossing their own rock onto the map of the United States.

2. Once a rock lands the player identifies the state they have landed on by marking it on their travel tracking sheet. Encourage players to name the specific state (Florida, Colorado, Minnesota, etc.). They can color it in with chalk (optional).

3. Game ends when all players have landed on each state, completing their journey around the United States of America.

Game Variations

★ Play game using a map of the continents.

★ Play game using a map of a country.

★ Play game using a map of a state or city.

I NEED IT

Needs and wants can be tough for young children to differentiate between. This can be evident in a trip to a toy store. Although it is okay to have wants, part of early childhood learning is to be able to separate the two. See if your child can identify the difference between something they need to survive and items that they want. Talk about how needs and wants may be similar or different in families all around the world.

 Focus Skill: distinguishing between needs and wants

Great for: on-the-go learning

Materials

Large sheet of paper

Red and blue markers

Pencil

Directions to Make

1. Write the word *WANT* in red and *NEED* in blue at the top of the paper.
2. Brainstorm a list of items children may need and want.
3. Need: food, shoes, clothing, shelter, backpack, school supplies.
4. Want: movie tickets, candy, new toys, coloring books.
5. Write these items in a list on the large sheet of paper.

Directions to Play

1. Hand two children the different-colored markers.
2. Read an item from the list. If the item is a want, the child holding the red marker gets to circle it. If it is a need, the child with the blue marker circles it.
3. If the child has circled a word or phrase, they pass their marker on to another player.
4. Play continues until all words and phrases have been circled.

Game Variations

★ Make a statement of want or need and encourage children to agree or disagree with it by showing a thumbs-up signal. I need toy cars = thumbs down.

★ Draw a picture of something you want on a piece of paper, a need on another piece. Assemble all the pictures into two separate kid-made books: I want... I need...

★ Read the item on the list. Have the children state whether they need or want it.

HOW MANY OF YOU?

Have you ever wondered how many of you it would take to reach the top of your house or even the Statue of Liberty? Players explore nonstandard measurement using their own height to compare to famous landmarks.

Focus Skill: identifying famous landmarks around the world

Materials

Photo image of child

5 sheets of paper for game pieces

2 sheets of paper for landmarks and height measurements

Directions to Make

1. Place multiple images of your child onto a Word document and print out. The image size should be 1 inch (2.5 cm) tall. Twenty-one images on five sheets of paper will provide enough game pieces.
2. Together search online to find images of famous landmarks to use for the game.
3. Write down how tall each chosen landmark is.
4. Print out images of landmarks with height and use as game pieces. Select four different structures per printed page.

Directions to Play

1. Each player chooses a famous landmark from the pile.
2. One player says "go" and each player works to re-create the size of the landmark using the game pieces.
3. The player that finishes first correctly wins that round.

Game Variations

★ Work together as a team to see how quickly you can measure the height of a famous landmark.

★ Sort the various landmarks by height.

★ Compare items around your house like your home, trees or car for players to learn on a smaller scale.

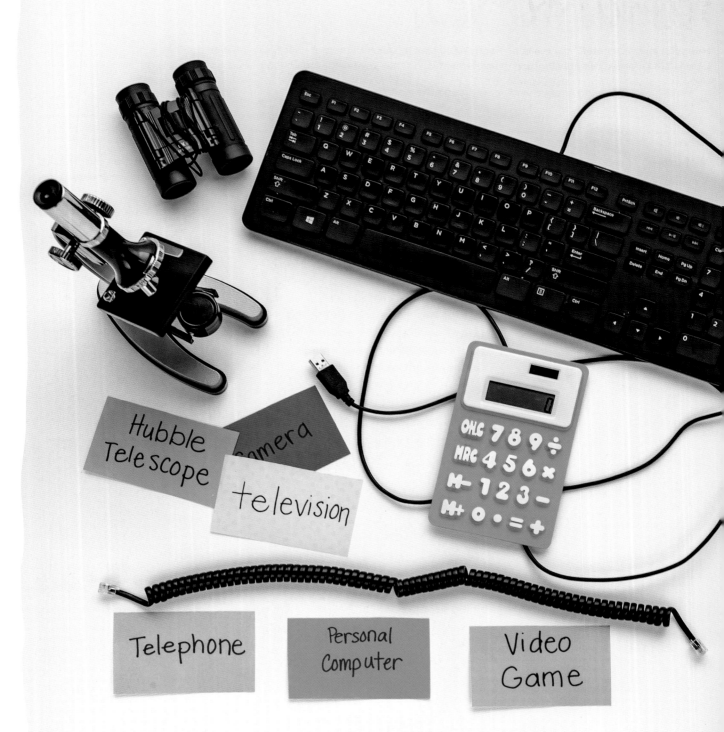

Hubble
Telescope

camera

television

Telephone

Personal
Computer

Video
Game

TECHNOLOGY TIMELINE

Technology plays a significant role in many young children's lives. Test your knowledge of the history of technology with this collaborative game to get kids thinking. Encourage children to talk about the significance of these technologies on their lives. Research using books and kid-friendly websites if help is needed!

Focus Skill: making a timeline of important events

Materials

3" x 5" (7.6 x 12.7-cm) notecards

Pencil

Directions to Make

1. Write a form of technology on each card: television, Hubble telescope, video game, telephone, camera, personal computer, etc.

Directions to Play

1. Hand the cards to the children. Read the words out loud.
2. Allow the group to arrange the cards in the order in which they think each was invented.
3. Check. Provide hints to help them change any technology items on their timeline.

Game Variations

★ Focus on specific inventors, scientific discoveries or forms of travel.

★ Let each player choose one item to learn more about prior to the game beginning. Allow them to be the expert and teach others about their technology invention.

★ Make a card for the dates and have children order the numbers and use dates on the inventions on the timeline as well.

Note

Don't show them these dates until after the game: 1876 telephone, 1888 camera, 1927 television, 1972 video game, 1983 personal computer, 1990 Hubble telescope.

ROLL A LANDFORM

What is that called? Players roll the dice to see what types of landforms they can match on the Earth. Many children live in an area with limited types of landforms. Children can use this game to discover others as they explore their world.

Focus Skill: identifying various types of landforms around the world

Materials

Square tissue box or homemade cardboard box (see page 72 for tutorial)

Construction paper

Markers or crayons

Scissors

Glue

2 pieces of paper

Pencil

Directions to Make

1. Create six images for the various types of landforms. Include mountain, lake, river, ocean, island, plateau, glacier, coast, canyon, plains, hill, valley or desert.

2. Attach images onto the side of the box.

3. Create a tally sheet with landform images.

Directions to Play

1. Players roll the box to identify a landform.

2. Once it lands, a player marks a tally mark on the recording form that corresponds to the matching landform.

3. The player who reaches six landforms first wins!

Game Variations

★ Focus images on types of bodies of water.

★ Focus images on types of mountains.

★ Create with images that feature types of environments.

CONTINENT FORTUNE-TELLER

Grab a partner and go global with this paper-folding fortune-teller game. Make your game board, then count and move for your challenge. Locate the continents on the map, refold the game board back together and count again! We know you will soon be able to identify all seven continents.

Focus Skill: identifying the seven continents

Materials

Square piece of paper

Pencil

Map or globe

Game Variations

★ Write famous landforms, major cities or important landmarks on the inside triangles.

★ Use this game to practice math facts. Write a number sentence on each triangle for kids to solve before moving back and forth.

★ Write sight words on each triangle. Move the fortune-teller the number of letters in the word. Write a sentence using that word on the inside for them to read out loud.

Directions to Make

1. Fold the square paper in half at both diagonals. Crease and unfold. Fold the square again at each middle. Unfold.

2. Bring each corner evenly to the middle of the square.

3. Flip the square over and fold the corners evenly into the middle of the square again.

4. Fold in half and flip over.

5. Place your fingers into the slits and open.

6. Open each triangle and write one of the following on each half: Find North America, Find South America, Point to Australia, Point to Europe, Find Asia, Find Africa, Point to Antarctica, Point and Name an Ocean.

7. To complete the fortune-teller, write numbers 1 to 8 on the inside triangles.

Directions to Play

1. Player one places their fingers in the fortune-teller and opens to show four numbers.

2. Player two picks one of the four numbers and player one moves the fortune-teller back and forth that many times.

3. Player two picks another number. Player one then opens the fortune-teller to read their task.

4. Player two completes the task using the map or globe.

5. The game repeats with player two holding the fortune-teller.

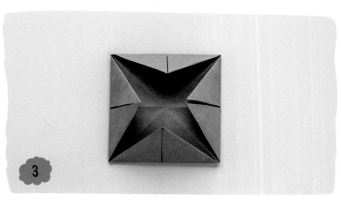

ACKNOWLEDGMENTS

We would like to say "thank you" to our family, friends and community for being so encouraging of our thoughts and ideas. To our spouses who have supported our late work nights, brainstormed with us and allowed us to bounce ideas off of you. To our children who have tested these learning games with us and assisted with photographs. To our parents who have read through the activities and have provided unwavering support of our successes in life.

Thank you to our amazing friends throughout the years who have attended our educational play dates and helped to bring this book to reality. From letting us "shop" your toys for props in the book to bringing your kids over to play—thank you.

To our online friends, we thank you for your continuing support and encouragement. To our readers at The Educators' Spin On It, thank you for reading, sharing and doing educational activities with your children. We hope this book brings you many memorable moments.

ABOUT THE AUTHORS

Amanda Boyarshinov is a National Board certified teacher with oodles of experience in early childhood education. She holds a bachelor's degree in elementary education and a master's degree in reading for grades K-12. You will often find her in her backyard exploring nature with her kids or doing a hands-on science project at the kitchen table.

Kim Vij is a certified teacher with over 20 years of experience teaching in early childhood education. She transitioned from classroom teaching to have a wider and stronger impact on early childhood education through advocacy. Her live and online appearances have helped her spread her message and become one of the leading experts of early childhood developmental activities. When she's not advising clients on developmentally appropriate strategies you can find her on Pinterest at www.pinterest.com/educatorsspinon.

Amanda and Kim are the co-founders of TheEducatorsSpinOnIt.com, where they encourage parents and teachers to make everyday moments into teachable opportunities. They help over one million parents find ways to encourage their children to explore, create, play and learn with their award-winning Pinterest boards.

INDEX

N

S

Y

Z

"I LOVE these tried & true ideas in bringing learning, discovery and inspiration into the home. *100 Fun & Easy Learning Games for Kids* is bursting with age appropriate activities that are easy to make and a delight to play. What a simple and stimulating way to encourage your children!"

—TRACI PAIGE JOHNSON, mom and maker of kids programming "Blues' Clues" (and voice of Blue),
"Super Why and Creative Galaxy" and founder of YUMMICO children's media company

"*100 Fun & Easy Learning Games for Kids* is an amazing collection of activities that teaches kids core skills in fun and engaging ways! I love how it takes activities and projects kids will love and ties an academic twist on them so they are learning through play and exploration. These activities will help prep your kids for a more formal educational setting, and as a kindergarten teacher I so appreciate that!"

—JENNIFER KADAR, kindergarten teacher, mom and creator of the popular blog Simply Kinder

"Filled with great hands-on activities that are both fun and educational, this book presents great new ways to help your kids learn new skills and have a blast while doing it!"

—SANDRA LIN, founder/CEO of Kiwi Crate Inc.

"As a mom to three kids, I'm always looking for fun educational ideas that my kids will actually want to play. Nearly all of the activities in this book can be done without having to run to the craft store—something I really appreciate! It's truly a game book for families."

—LAURA FUENTES, founder of MOMables.com

"*100 Fun & Easy Learning Game for Kids* helps parents by providing ideas, inspiration as well as the educational benefits behind it all. Kim and Amanda know how to strike the right balance for activities that are fun but can be done with a parent and child at home. Family game night just got much more fun... and educational!"

—ALLISON MCDONALD, preschool teacher, founder of No Time for Flash Cards
and author of *Raising A Rock-Star Reader*

"*100 Fun & Easy Learning Games for Kids* is a must-have for parents and teachers everywhere! It is packed with ideas on how to turn recyclables and everyday materials into learning games that kids love to play."

—ANNIE DOUGLASS, director of the online community Moms Meet

"Kim and Amanda consistently create wonderfully creative and fun educational activities for kids. Because they are moms and teachers, they get it: their supply list is easily obtainable and affordable, their activities are based on play and their educational twist is a nice bonus. This is all parents need to keep little ones entertained while preparing them for elementary school."

—MIA WENJEN, children's book blogger and co-founder of Multicultural Children's Book Day

"As a homeschooling parent I like to keep educational activities as fun as possible. This book is a go-to resource in our home because the games are easy to set up and we usually have all the supplies on hand!"

—VANESSA VARGAS WILSON, homeschooling mom and founder/CEO of Crafty Gemini

"What more could a parent ask for than a book packed with educational and engaging activities that are easy to prepare and fun to play together? Kim and Amanda bring their experience and passion for parenting and teaching to this must-have book. There's no better way to connect with your child than through learning and laughter."

—GISELLE SHARDLOW, author of *Kids Yoga Stories*